K.D. LANG: CARRYING THE TORCH

*"This is the way you pour yourself
into torch and twang: absolutely."*

k.d. lang

CARRYING THE TORCH

A biography by William Robertson

ECW PRESS

Copyright © ECW PRESS, 1992, 1993

CANADIAN CATALOGUING IN PUBLICATION DATA

Robertson, William
k.d. lang : carrying the torch

ISBN 1-55022-158-2

1. Lang, K.D., 1961–   . 2. Country musicians
– Canada – Biography. 1. Title.

ML420.L35R63 1992   782.42164'2'092   C92-094523-6

Design and imaging by ECW Type & Art, Oakville, Ontario.
Printed by Imprimerie Gagné, Louiseville, Québec.

Distributed in Canada by General Publishing Co. Limited,
30 Lesmill Road, Toronto, Ontario M3B 2T6
(416) 445-3333, (800) 387-0172 (Canada), FAX (416) 445-5967

Distributed to the trade in the United States exclusively by
INBOOK, 140 Commerce Street, P.O. Box 120261,
East Haven, Connecticut, U.S.A. 06512
(203) 467-4257, FAX (203) 469-7697
Customer service: 1-800-253-3605 or 1-800-243-0138

Published by ECW PRESS,
1980 Queen Street East, Toronto, Ontario M4L 1J2
(416) 694-3348

ACKNOWLEDGEMENTS

I wish to thank Kathy Naylor, Stephen Heatley, Nola Augustson, Wayne Gunnlaugson, and Jim Hodges for their time and reminiscences. I also wish to thank Wendy Schissel, Pamela Haig, and Linda McCann for introductions and reminders. Also, thanks to Larry Wanagas for his time and valuable help and big thanks to Janet Macko at Bumstead Productions for her help and patience. Thanks to the staffs of the London Public Library, the Fred Landon Branch Library, and the D.B. Weldon Library at the University of Western Ontario, and to those at the Frances Morrison Branch of the Saskatoon Public Library, the Murray Memorial Library at the University of Saskatchewan, and to Miriam Clemence and Ann Findlay at the library of the *StarPhoenix*. A special thanks to Bette Sadoway, Terry Craig, Michael Bourgeois, and to Rod and Jean Macpherson. Special thanks, as well, to Jack Trieber at the village office in Consort, Alberta, to Larry Kjearsgaard at Consort School, and to Bette Reichert at Frontier Photos in Saskatoon. A humdinger of a thanks to Susan Gingell, and to Lee and Carrie Beckmann, ever vigilant at the TV.

Cover photo, 1991, Albert Sanchez © 1991 Visages, is used by permission of Visages; frontispiece illustration, 1991, Peggy Sirota, is used by permission of the photographer; illustration 2, 1984, Tom Braid and Perry Mah/*Alberta Report*, is used by permission of United Western Communications Ltd.; illustration 3, © 1986 Jim Reichert, is used by permission of Frontier Photos; illustration 4, 1979, Pat Jacobsen, and illustrations 6 (1978), 7 (1979), and 8 (1979) are used by permission of Consort School; illustration 5, © 1986, is used by permission of the Village of Consort Office; illustration 9, 1984, is used by permission of Bumstead Productions Ltd.; illustration 10, 1984, Tom Braid and Perry Mah/*Alberta Report*, is used by permission of United Western Communication Ltd.; illustration 11, 1985, *Toronto Star*, is used by permission of Canada Wide Feature Service Ltd.; illustrations 12 and 13, 1987, Victoria Pearson, are used by permission of the photographer; illustration 14, 1988, Stuart Watson, is used by permission of the photographer; illustration 15, 1988, Paul Till, is used by permission of the photographer; illustration 16, 1989, *StarPhoenix* [Saskatoon], is used by permission of the *StarPhoenix*; illustration 17, 1992, Edie Baskin, is used by permission of Onyx Enterprises Inc.

ECW PRESS wishes to acknowledge the assistance of Margery Fee, a consultant to the Canadian Biography Series.

TABLE OF CONTENTS

LIST OF ILLUSTRATIONS

A NOTE ON THE TEXT

Because Kathy Lang has chosen to call herself k.d. lang, but was not k.d. lang until the early 1980s, I have tailored my presentation of her name to the way she would have written it at the time.

Not everyone appreciated, or, perhaps more accurately, could figure out, her approach to substituting lowercase letters for the conventional uppercase in proper names. For whatever reason, many journalists, newspapers, and magazines have resolutely refused to use any but conventional spelling. I have quoted from printed material as it appears, not as lang would have written her name herself.

Also, I have put no comma in the title *Red Hot + Blue* as that is how it appears on the cover of the CD. The disk itself is labelled *Red, Hot & Blue*, while *Time* magazine takes a middle path: *Red, Hot + Blue*. I went with the way *Musician* magazine quoted Ben Mink on the subject.

Chronology

1961   Kathryn Dawn Lang born 2 November in Edmonton, fourth of four children, to Audrey and Fred Lang.

1962   The Langs move to Consort, Alberta, where Fred Lang opens Lang's Pharmacy.

1963   Patsy Cline, with whom k.d. lang will later claim a major spiritual connection, dies in an air crash on 5 March in Camden, Tennessee.

1968   Kathy Lang studies piano at Theresetta Convent, Castor, Alberta.

1973   Her parents split up, she stays with her mother, brother, and sisters.

1974   Gets her first guitar.

1975   Writes her first song, "Hoping My Dreams Come True."

1977   First paid performance, Consort Kinsmen Club's Las Vegas Casino Night; sings three songs for $25.

1979   Ranked eighth in Canada in javelin throw. Graduates from high school and enrolls in the music program at Red Deer College.

1981   Opens for Holly Wright at the Provincial Museum in Edmonton (13 November). Lands a part in Theatre Network/Red Deer College's *Country Chorale*.

1983   Answers an ad for a singer in a Texas swing band in Edmonton and meets Larry Wanagas. Signs management and publishing agreement with Wanagas. Becomes "k.d. lang." Records her first single, "Friday Dance Promenade."

1984   Her good friend Drifter (Gary Elgar) dies in Red Deer. Records and releases *a truly western experience*. Hits big at the Edmonton Folk Festival (August). Begins first cross-Canada tour.

1985   American debut at New York's Bottom Line (May). Signs recording contract with Seymour Stein of Sire Records (summer). Meets Ben Mink. Accepts first Juno Award wearing a wedding dress (4 November).

1986   Records *Angel with a Lariat* in London with Dave Edmunds (May–June).

1987   *Angel with a Lariat* released. Starts work on *Shadowland* in Nashville with Owen Bradley. Plays the Grand Ole Opry (October).

1988   Named *Chatelaine* magazine's Woman of the Year. Leads square dance at Calgary Winter Games closing ceremonies (February). *Shadowland* released. Starts work on *Absolute Torch and Twang* in Vancouver.

1989   Wins first Grammy Award for "Crying," Best Country Vocal Collaboration, with Roy Orbison. *Absolute Torch and Twang* released. Films *k.d. lang's Buffalo Cafe*.

1990   Shoots ad for People for the Ethical Treatment of Animals (PETA) in Los Angeles and creates furore in Alberta. Records "Ridin' the Rails" for *Dick Tracy* soundtrack. Records "So in Love" in Vancouver for *Red Hot + Blue*, a multi-artist, Cole Porter commemorative, and AIDS awareness album. Begins filming *Salmonberries* with Percy Adlon.

1991   Begins work on *Ingénue* in Vancouver. *Salmonberries* premieres at Montréal World Film Festival and wins Best Film award (September). Wins Female Artist of the Decade award (20 November). Video collection *k.d. lang: Harvest of Seven Years (Cropped and Chronicled)* released.

1992   *Ingénue* released (17 March). Declares she is a lesbian in a cover story and interview with *The Advocate* (16 June).

k.d. lang

CARRYING THE TORCH

"HI THERE, BOBS AND BETTYS!" That's what she called us when she ran onto stage and grabbed the microphone — Bobs and Bettys. And what an outfit! Those glasses. That hair. And what'd she done to those boots?!

The first time I saw k.d. lang was at a dance at the Western Development Museum on the south edge of Saskatoon, Saskatchewan. It was April 1985.

I'd been living in Ontario for about a year and when I got back to Saskatoon a concert promoter friend of mine told me I had to go see k.d. lang, she was causing a sensation. I'd never heard of her, but as a concert and record reviewer for Saskatoon's *StarPhoenix*, I'd heard my friend speak of "sensations" many times before. In fact, when he told me she was the hottest thing in Canadian country music, I thought he said "Katie Lang."

By the time I stood in a long lineup a couple of months later, waiting to get into the Western Development Museum, I'd had a chance to wonder what "Katie Lang" would be like. In what way could a person be a "hot new sensation" in country music?

I had something of a prejudice against country music — or what I still called country and western, at that time — born of working in my late teens and early twenties in a small-town garage where the radio got only one station, the local C & W one. To me country was all rednecks singing about whiskey and how longhairs should stop complaining about the Vietnam war, and it was women with their hair piled high, wailing that they'd stick with their man no matter what kind of a mean drunk he was. Not pretty stuff.

Up until a few days before the dance I thought Lang's options were to take the long-suffering route, like Tammy Wynette, standing by her man; the goofball comic route, like Minnie Pearl, screeching "HOW-Deee" from the stage of the Grand Ole Opry; or perhaps, and for this I hoped, the new "progressive traditionalist" route, like Emmylou Harris, who had a clear voice and even threw in a little rock and roll from people like Chuck Berry.

Three days before the dance I got my tickets and learned how to spell k.d. lang. Not "Katie," or Tammy or Kitty or Dolly or Loretta, but, as Stompin' Tom Connors would later instruct us: "Little k, little d, little l-a-n-g. . . ." This revelation threw a curve into my thinking. She spelled her name in the same style as American poet e.e. cummings, or Canadian poets bill bissett and bpNichol. You can't spell your name in such an openly rebellious manner and sing traditional, or at least Nashville establishment, country music. That left comedy. Maybe she was a comedian. But cummings, bissett, and Nichol aren't comedians, I thought. Or are they?

Once inside I staked out a corner of a long, Legion Hall-style table and got a look at the stage. It was framed with piping to hold the lights, as usual, but hanging from one of the pipes was a child's plastic riding horse. Hanging from the horse's head was a bizarre mane that looked, from where I sat, like a captured mop-head. On the stage itself stood a lamp, which was switched on, with a small end-table beside it. On the table sat a big, glass ashtray.

By now the hall was crowded and alive with the kind of dull roar that precedes a concert. And what a crowd. I'd been to rock concerts by the likes of Styx and Prism where I'd felt like the oldest guy in the building, country concerts by Waylon Jennings and Charlie Pride where I could barely see the stage for all the brand new cowboy hats, and blues concerts where there could always be had a curious mix of earnest-looking intellectuals, musicians bopping along to their own rhythm track, and a phalanx of burly bikers, arms crossed, grimly awaiting satis-faction.

When it came to curious mixes, though, lang had them all beat. The boppers were here, the country crowd in hats and

FIGURE 2

k.d. lang: A truly western experience.

shiny boots, bikers, ten-speeders, musicians, the local theatre crowd, artists, the whole-grain people, folks in tweed jackets, and the gangs that scoured the city, rooting out alternative music. The word had gotten round, and people being what they are, they'd heard what they wanted to hear about k.d. lang and now sat in a wild assortment of anticipation.

Out came an emcee with his usual patter about who brought us the show. Then he introduced the reclines, lang's backup band. They launched into a spirited tune to get us even more revved up, then this wild woman who had to be k.d. lang burst onto the stage and started to belt out her opening number.

I can't remember the song. I was not there in my capacity as a concert reviewer, nor was anyone else from the city paper, as the entertainment editor had not deemed a dance way out at the museum fuelled by an unknown artist worthy of review, so I kept no record. What mattered to me and everyone else who leapt to the dance floor in one exuberant whoosh was the whole feast of sensations k.d. lang produced.

The music was rollicking and happy, with a tight rhythm section driving it along. Cavorting in front of it, lang looked like nothing we'd ever seen before. She had the spiky haircut of a punk or new-waver, cat's-eye glasses with no lenses in them, a cowgirl skirt with what looked like little cowboys and Indians sewn onto it, a western shirt, and on her feet, a pair of what were once black cowboy boots, sawed off just above ankle level, showing the tops of a pair of classic, red-trimmed wool socks. I didn't know quite what to make of this vision.

The punk haircut seemed to thumb its nose at any established music industry, country particularly. The glasses seemed to poke fun at lang herself, and at the fifties from which they came, all the while harking back to that era. The skirt referred back to the same era, though not even a Dale Evans or a Rose Maddox would ever again be caught in such a thing as this, especially with the little cowboys and Indians dancing along its sides, making a big joke of cowgirl skirts. The shirt was all man, while the boots were like a stab into the heart of manliness, especially prairie manliness.

Who in their right mind, male or female, would savagely saw the tops off a pair of cowboy boots, even if they were old and ready for boot hill? If she wanted a pair of Beatle-boots, why not just go dig up a pair at a thrift store? No, these were definitely cowboy boots that had been abused and were now being flaunted as such in the Canadian heart of cowboy-boot country. And the socks? Unrepentant local hippies could still be seen wearing these wool numbers in their now out-of-style work boots and their in-style Birkenstock sandals. Just whose side was she on, anyway?

This urgency to categorize that plagues the human animal was temporarily shoved aside by another need the human animal less often acknowledges, the one to dance. The reclines were partly responsible for that urgency, but lang's voice did the big job. She kicked down the doors of people's inhibitions by looking weirder and wilder than any of them had imagined. She kicked down the doors of their hearts with her soaring, swooping alto, the kind of voice that made even the most puzzled or offended members of the audience forgive and forget as they danced out of themselves and into the palms of lang's hands.

When lang romped through the old Webb Pierce/Mel Tillis rockabilly number "Bopalena," she sounded like an archivist with heart, a researcher determined to dig up old gold, dust it off, polish it up, and let it shine for a whole new audience. When she grabbed the mane off the toy horse's head, draped it over her own, and strutted the stage singing the old Nancy Sinatra hit "These Boots Are Made for Walking," she became a new-wave rocker with the quirky sense of humour inherent in new wave's form. What was serious, even sadistic, in 1966, pulled in lots of laughs nineteen years later.

These campy satiric jabs had even more effect in lang's treatment of Joanie Sommers's one big hit, "Johnny Get Angry." If ever a song demanded reassessment by a post-second wave feminist generation, it was this number from 1962. To the near-urgent tinklings of the piano, lang paced the stage and wrung her hands — obviously a girl with a problem. Then she started to sing: "Every girl wants someone who / She knows she can look up to. . . ." Members of the audience who in 1962 were either not yet born or too young to listen to the radio could hardly believe their ears. You could see something of a shocked delight on their faces as they stared at lang, wondering where this song came from and what its singer was up to.

After singing a plaintive first verse about what girls all need from their men, lang shifted her voice and her antics into high gear for the chorus:

Johnny get angry
Johnny get mad
Give me the biggest lecture I've ever had
I want a brave man
I want a cave man
Johnny show me that you care, really care
for me.

Wow! Who could believe these lyrics? And while she sang them, lang flung herself about the stage as if she were taking a beating from Johnny, a message no one could miss.

Around the second or third chorus lang took such a shot on the jaw from her loving neanderthal that she flew off the stage into the middle of the dance floor, scattering the dancers.

There she lay, face down, not moving a muscle. Now what? The nervous piano tinkled on. After a good thirty seconds, during which many of the now-motionless dancing crowd almost gave her a tentative prod with a foot, a low moan was uttered from lang's prostrate body. The moan became a wail, grew louder, then mounted and mounted in intensity till we all thought she'd died and come back as an operatic diva. What was that she was wailing?

J-o-h-h-h-h-n-n-n-n-y-y-y-y-y-y-y

and she sprang to her feet, microphone still in hand, ran and leapt back onstage to finish the number. The crowd went wild.

This was satire, guerilla theatre, and feminism all rolled up in a blast from the past, played well and sung even better. But lang wasn't about to cast herself completely into the heavily drenched ironies of the waiting new-wave crowd. Somewhere in the hype for this show the word country was mentioned and lang liberally spiked her sets with polkas and square dances, calling some of the steps herself, or getting a band member to do so while she gave the audience a demonstration.

Then with lights lowered, but lamp shining dully, lang assumed a serious posture and sang "Three Cigarettes in an Ashtray." That she sang to the ashtray in her hand would have told most witnesses that she just couldn't get her tongue out of her cheek, but for the fact of her voice again. What she gave to the theatre of "Johnny Get Angry," she gave all and more of to the singing of this old heartbreaker from the late Patsy Cline.

Here was country music so traditional it went back to the fifties and early sixties and, in the case of the polkas and square dances, much earlier.

People I spoke to, both at the dance and as we staggered out to the parking lot, soaked with sweat, didn't care a whit where lang belonged in a musical categorization. Whether she was Nashville country, new-wave rock, roots rockabilly, old-time country hoedown, blues, western swing, or jazz — all areas she'd worked through that evening — wasn't an issue. When lang took the stage earlier she'd proclaimed, "Hi there, Bobs and Bettys. We're gonna have a rootin', tootin', wing-dang-daddy-o of a good time tonight," and we sure enough did.

In the intervening years, most everyone concerned with the music business has been trying to figure out just where they can put k.d. lang. But she's had ideas of her own.

Consort: Portrait of The Singer as Tomboy

she was a big boned gal
from southern alberta
you just couldn't call her small

(k.d. lang/Ben Mink "Big Boned Gal")

Kathryn Dawn Lang was born 2 November 1961, in Edmonton, Alberta. She is the fourth child of Audrey and Fred Lang, the former a teacher and the latter a pharmacist. Her brother, John, was eleven when she was born and her sisters Jo Ann and Keltie, six and three, respectively.

FIGURE 3

An aerial view of Consort, Alberta, population 650.

When Kathy was six months old, the Lang family moved to the small farming community of Consort, Alberta (present population, approximately 650), where her father opened Lang's Pharmacy and her mother eventually taught grade two at the local school.

Consort is a typical prairie town in that its main street, called 50th, is home to such businesses as Consort Foods, Meter Variety, the Consort Hotel, and the Consort Dining Lounge (Chinese & Western Cuisine), while its few, mainly residential, secondary streets lead to the Consort District Sportplex, the Consort Municipal Hospital, several churches, the RCMP office, and the Alberta Liquor Store. There's also the standard service road and railway tracks where the grain elevators are lined up, these three all bearing the dull green of the Alberta Wheat Pool.

Atypically, the grain elevators don't give Consort the prairie skyline familiar to most Canadians. Consort is built on the side of a hill that runs down to a small creek, and it's here that the railway runs and the elevators have to be. Standing in the middle of Consort one can look down the hill, across the highway, and over the tops of the elevators to the hills on the other side of the valley. On top of them is a distinctive Alberta landmark: a nest of oil pumpjacks and storage tanks, plus a tall burn-off stack for gas with its perpetual flame flickering on the southern horizon. At the northwest end of town there's another burn-off stack, so at night the community is nestled between two high flames.

Consort is located on Highway 12, about 225 kilometers due east of Red Deer and 60 kilometers west of the Saskatchewan border. Once into Saskatchewan, Alberta Highway 12 becomes Saskatchewan Highway 51 and takes something of a crooked route 248 kilometers to Saskatoon. All these numbers mean Consort is a few hours' car ride from any city and separated from neighbours like Veteran and Throne to the west and Provost to the north by large tracts of cattle-grazing country, mixed grain farmland, lots of small aspen and poplar stands full of deer, and beneath it all, oil and natural gas.

What you have then for people are ranchers and farmers, a few of whom turn to rodeoing when the warm weather comes back and the professional rodeos start making their circuits; oil field workers, who occasionally drill new wells but mostly maintain the existing pumpjacks, seesawing the crude out of the ground; and the townspeople who have congregated around these industries. They all live and work in the gentle moraines that make up the Neutral Hills, an aboriginal neutral zone where the once warring Cree and Blackfoot tribes could come to hunt in peace. The local newspaper, the *Consort Enterprise*, calls itself, appropriately, "The Voice of the Neutrals."

The Young Eccentric

Newspaper and magazine articles have flooded forth with the rising popularity of k.d. lang. If those articles say anything about her years in Consort, the singer-to-be is often described with adjectives such as "unconventional," "unique," "eccentric," and "bohemian." Her mother is quoted in one article as saying, "Kathy had an entertainer's flair from the age of two. She always got the spotlight. She had boundless energy. She never was swayed by what others did" (Gillmor 33). That last statement, particularly, is of note in the small-town context. To stand out from the crowd when the crowd is small, relatively remote, and pushed by the two extremes of the frigid Canadian prairie winter and the baking prairie summer is no small feat.

Bohemians and unconventional types can exist anywhere, but in a small rural community, which many people who come from such places compare to living in a fishbowl, those eccentrics stick out far more than they would in a city. For some sensitive people, their perceived oddness can be crushing. They don't look and act like everyone else, they're hounded for it, and they get out and stay out at the earliest possible opportunity. Some so-called oddball types are more fortunate. Their weirdness may be challenged, but their inner strength and/or the nurturing proximity of their family and close friends is there to back them up and help them rise to the occasion.

Kathy Lang appears to have been one of the fortunate ones, and now is quick to defend the small town from charges that it's hostile to eccentricity:

I have a theory that small towns, because they are small, because there are 650 people and because you know them for 17 years, that those people just become eccentrics that you know. That's k.d. lang, that's Bill Holms who drives his tractor to school, and that's [the guy] who gets drunk every Saturday night on Aqua Velva. Those are the people that live in your home, those are the people that live in your neighbourhood, and in the city you have more ways to shut yourself off from eccentrics. You can pass them on the street and never see that person again. You don't have to go to church with them on Sunday. You know what I mean, you can close yourself off. Where in a small town you know them and you know them for 25–30 years. ("k.d. lang Interview" 12)

The strength to defy the odds, she acknowledges in a 1990 *Glamour* article, came from Audrey and Fred Lang: "My parents brought me up with no limitations. They supported my self-confidence and never said, 'Only boys can do that.' I rode motorcycles. I played sports. I did whatever I wanted to" (Krupp).

One of Kathy Lang's earliest ambitions was to be a roller-derby queen. To practise she would strap on her skates and scoot up and down the aisles of her father's store. Another thing she practised at the store was shooting. Fred Lang, according to a *Saturday Night* article, called her his "boy-girl" and taught her how to shoot: "[A]t twelve she had her own shotgun. She and her father would lie down at the front door of the family drugstore and shoot through to a target in the dispensary at the back. They went to shooting matches together, and Kathy often returned with prizes" (Gillmor 33).

She was also the first girl in Consort to own a motorcycle, and friend and former teacher Kathy Naylor remembers Lang with a dirt bike. *Starsky and Hutch*, a television program about two handsome Californian policemen, was popular at the time, and one of Lang's favourites. "She wanted to be like them," says Naylor. "Another of her ambitions was to be a policewoman and she'd roar around town on that bike playing cop."

The supreme confidence that would later take her through

and out of Consort and onto world stages remained relatively intact despite the breakup of her parents' marriage in 1973, giving further proof of the solid sense of self she developed as a young girl. Don Gillmor portrays the event most poignantly in his *Saturday Night* article when he writes that Lang's father "left the year Kathy was twelve, lighting out in the spirit of western divorce." He goes on to quote Audrey Lang, who adds, "When he left, he left. I don't know where he lives, I truly don't. I don't think any of the kids know either" (33). *Chatelaine* magazine notes that up until the time of the split, Kathy believed the family was close and that since the split her relationship with her mother "gets better and better" (Scott 132). In 1992 k.d. lang told the *Advocate* that she was sure her feelings of aloneness as an adult were "because my father left the family when I was 12, and my teenage years were my mother and I" (Lemon 40). She told *Us* magazine the same year that her father abandoned the family and that the event was "a huge trauma, mostly because it hurt my mother so much, and I hated seeing her hurt. He just vanished. I've talked to him three times since then" (McKenna 50).

Young adolescence, as most people are painfully aware, is a time of wild growth and rigid adherence to unwritten and constantly shifting codes. Many will admit, once through it, that one of its predominant emotions is fear. Fear of doing, saying, or wearing the wrong thing; of having one's parent do, say, or wear the wrong thing. Kathy Lang, with a confidence born of strong encouragement from her family, took two sure routes to survival through and out of adolescence: music and sports.

The Musical Route

Soon after the Lang family moved to Consort in 1962, Audrey Lang bought a second-hand Mason and Risch piano in Edmonton and used her family-allowance cheques to make the monthly payments.

When Kathy was seven her mother began taking her and her brother, John, to Castor, straight west on Highway 12. The one-hour car ride brought them to the Theresetta Convent where they took piano lessons from Sister Xavier, one of the last of a Catholic order called the Daughters of Wisdom. An *Alberta Report* article quotes Kathy's former teacher as saying, "She had a pretty voice even then" (Philip, Whyte, and Cohen 39). Though Kathy apparently had little desire to practise, the time was hardly wasted. While she sat in the convent waiting for her brother to finish his lesson and listened to him going over his scales, she says, "that was where I got my ear" (Philip, Whyte, and Cohen 39).

Saturday Night reports that in her first year of lessons Kathy was asked by Sister Xavier if she would like to sing at a music festival in the town of Coronation, halfway between Castor and Consort. Her response was brief but emphatic: "Oh, could I?" (Gillmor 32).

When interviewed by early sixties singing star Lesley Gore for *Ms.* magazine, Lang and the singer of such hits as "It's My Party" and "You Don't Own Me" compared notes on their early musical fantasies:

> LESLEY: When did you know you had to be a singer?
> k.d.: Always. My siblings and I studied classical piano for years. I sang in school, in competitions, around.
> LESLEY: As a child I wanted to sing at Carnegie Hall, so I practiced singing behind the closed bedroom door, in front of the full-length mirror, with a hairbrush as my microphone.
> k.d.: I definitely practiced in front of the full-length mirror. But not behind closed doors, god, no! I wanted an audience all the time. (lang, "Lesley Gore" 30)

Obviously Sister Xavier was right on the button. She taught Kathy a short song and she practised it there at the convent. Said Sister Xavier: "The tears came to my eyes when I heard her sing" (Gillmor 32). Years later Sister Xavier is still moved by Kathy Lang's voice. She told *Saturday Night*, "She has wonderful breath control. She can hold a note until the cows come home. So to speak" (Gillmor 33).

Meanwhile, back home in Consort, Kathy had her ears wide open, listening, listening, listening. The Lang children had an old Seabreeze record player, and she and her sister Keltie would take in Creedence Clearwater Revival, Eric Clapton, Maria Muldaur, and Joe Cocker, all of it rock and roll. As she's told many an interviewer, the country music would come later; for now there were the Allman Brothers.

In one day Kathy Lang could hear Creedence belt out "Fortunate Son," Joe Cocker with his Mad Dogs and Englishmen rasp and rattle their way through "Delta Lady," then she could move on to a clear-eyed and inspirational "Climb Every Mountain" by Julie Andrews, as favoured by her mother, and hear Percy Faith sweep through his own orchestral pop versions of such recent hits as "Que Sera Sera" and "Love Is Blue," as favoured by her father. Before she headed out the door she could tune into one of her favourite TV shows, *The Beverly Hillbillies* ("They influenced me a lot; they were so honest compared to their surroundings" [Philip, Whyte, and Cohen 39]), and hear Lester Flatt and Earl Scruggs do the theme song with some high-spirited bluegrass picking on the banjo and guitar. Then, she could cap the evening with a trip to a wedding dance where she'd hear an old-time country quartet (drums, guitar, accordion, and saxophone, for instance) mix it up with polkas, schottisches, two-steps, and waltzes that went by such names as "The Too-Fat Polka," "In the Finnish Woods," "The Peek-a-Boo Waltz," and "Under the Double Eagle." Quite a mix of eras, styles, and tempos.

Somewhere in there she probably caught a couple of rides with people who had their radios tuned to the local country station. Either that or she went to the café and caught some country tunes on the jukebox — songs like "Don't Come Home a' Drinkin' (with Lovin' on Your Mind)" by Loretta Lynn, "A Boy Named Sue" by Johnny Cash, "D-I-V-O-R-C-E" by Tammy Wynette, "Okie from Muskogee" by Merle Haggard, or perhaps another song from that era and a giant hit for Lynn Anderson, "Rose Garden."

When Kathy was ten she'd had enough of piano lessons and quit, "frustrated with daily practising and unwilling to follow the notes as they were written on the page" (Gillmor 33), which fits well, of course, with the eccentric image she was cultivating around town and with the image she would later project in the music world. Soon after — some sources say at age twelve, others say thirteen — she did what countless other young teenagers have done when they've left what they feel are the stultifying confines of that huge, hulking instrument, the piano, and its regimented weekly lessons. She got herself a guitar.

Now guitars were fervently appropriated by the first rock and roll generation of the fifties and early sixties as a symbol of mobility, defiance, romance, and sexual prowess. Guitars had been taken from such sources as country (through pickers like Merle Travis), folk (through strummers like Woody Guthrie), and blues (through the guitar magic of Leadbelly and the mysterious Robert Johnson, who supposedly sold his soul to the devil for his ability to play). Because of this almost holy (or unholy) aura that hangs over the guitar, it's not surprising that Kathy Lang picked one up, especially considering the "entertainer's flair" her mother credited her with having, nor is it surprising that the origins of her first guitar (or guitars) are already shrouded in mystery.

According to a 1984 *Alberta Report* article, Kathy bought her first guitar at age thirteen: a twelve-string Yamaha (Philip, Whyte, and Cohen 39). In the *Canadian Composer*, a year later, the reading public was told that she had stolen her brother's guitar (Flohil, "Voice" 6), while in a more recent article, *Saturday Night* said an older sister had a guitar and that Kathy just picked it up (Gillmor 33). Playing on the jumble of information, Tom Hawthorn opened his article on Lang in *This Magazine* with this fanciful description of the musician's first guitar:

> She was handed a guitar by a drifting cowboy at a tender age, taught herself how to play while strumming along to live radio broadcasts from the Grand Ole Opry and hasn't missed an episode of *Hee-Haw* since it replaced the censored *Smothers Brothers Comedy Hour* way back in the hot summer of 1969. (12)

It doesn't take long for the stories to go round and for people to hear what they want to hear. The article in the *Canadian Composer* had as one of its subtitles, "The Legend Grows," and what becomes a legend most is the forgetting of certain facts and the incorporating of other, better "facts." Kathy Naylor says that when she and her husband moved to Consort in 1975, Lang already had a six-string guitar and would bring it over to Naylor's house to play with her husband, Rob. When Lang was in grade ten, Naylor accompanied Audrey Lang on a shopping expedition to Calgary to buy the younger Kathy a twelve-string.

Even if these tales can't all be true, the point is they are all doing their part in turning k.d. lang into a legend in her own time. Above all, they indicate she most certainly laid hands on a guitar in her early teens. Many articles on Lang emphasize that she was never far from her guitar during her later school years. Naylor adds that Lang became a regular visitor to her home, learning new songs from Rob, trying out others on her captive audience, and generally honing her skills as a player and a singer. The need for an audience she mentioned to Lesley Gore in the *Ms.* interview found its outlet in various functions around town, including weddings, school socials, and talent contests. She also took the guitar along on school-team road trips, and Larry Kjearsgaard, principal at Consort School, is quoted in *Alberta Report* as saying, "Those trips were never dull. I'll always remember Kathy sitting in the back of the bus belting out *That'll Be The Day*" (Philip, Whyte, and Cohen 39). The same article reports Lang's own recollection of one trip in which she "suddenly realized a talent contest was underway at that moment in nearby Coronation. After persuading the bus driver to make the necessary detour, 'I just walked in, still in my bright yellow track suit, sang, won, and left'" (39).

Another road trip on which Kathy took her guitar was one to the east coast. In grade nine, when she was fourteen, a teacher originally from Nova Scotia took the girls on a basketball trip to Halifax. Naylor, who wasn't along on the trip, claims Kathy wrote her first song, "Hoping My Dreams Come True," while she was gone. According to *Alberta Report*, Lang "even sent some lyrics to Anne Murray, adding an ingenuous P.S.: 'You are permitted to use my lyrics.' (The singer never wrote back, nor did she use the material)" (Philip, Whyte, and Cohen 39). Naylor also recalls that Kathy was a student who could have done better in school but "instead of doing her homework, she wrote songs. All she wanted to do was sing and perform."

Kathy's first paid performance was at the Consort Kinsmen

FIGURE 4

Kathy Lang singing the grade twelve graduation
theme song she wrote, "The End of Our Beginning."

Consort

Alberta

FIGURE 5

The sign erected to welcome visitors to Consort, Alberta.

Club's Las Vegas Casino Night in 1977. She got up with her twelve-string guitar, sang three numbers, and earned $25. Naylor remembers, as well, that Kathy wrote and sang the theme song for her grade twelve graduation ("The End of Our Beginning") and that she entered a song in the Alberta Youth Talent Search.

It becomes evident from the testimony of people in her past that no matter how supposedly meteoric k.d. lang's rise to fame, particularly in Canada, a young woman named Kathy Lang had her mind set on something bigger for herself than sing-alongs in the back of the school bus and did a lot of work preparing herself for a future in the entertainment business. In the Consort School's 1979 yearbook Kathy Lang claimed to be heading for a career in music and the town of Consort eventually erected a sign welcoming visitors to the "Home of k.d. lang."

The Sports Route

Besides the strong encouragement she got from her family and the rewards brought by her love of music and her increasing ability to listen, sing, and play, Kathy must have drawn considerable strength from her commitment to sports. Of course, like anything else, it was a two-way street: she gave to it and it gave back.

Kathy is quoted in an *Alberta Report* article as saying, "I lived for sports. Especially volleyball. When you live in a small town and you're not a boy and don't play hockey, there's not much else to do" (Philip, Whyte, and Cohen 39). The truth is, Kathy Lang found plenty to do.

Kathy Naylor, her high school basketball coach, claims Kathy was a fine athlete. "She was a big girl, and very strong. She wasn't really coordinated, but her strength overcame that lack." That strength obviously overcame the lack enough to allow Lang to rise above the demands of the game and exercise her other love. "Kathy would get a breakaway and be going for the basket," says Naylor, "and be singing all the way. Nothing bothered her."

FIGURE 6

*Kathy Lang in grade eleven with Consort School's senior
girls basketball team. Lang is seated, second from right,
and coach Kathy Naylor is next to her on the far right.*

Well, almost nothing. Naylor also remembers one other incident, a rather unfortunate one for Kathy. She had braces on her
teeth at the time and at a high-school volleyball tournament
went up for a spike and came down, braces first, into the net.
Then came the job of untangling her.

Besides all those tournaments and away games where she
took her guitar and entertained on the road, Kathy also developed her skills with the javelin and in 1979 she was ranked
eighth in Canada.

Add to the musical and sporting skills a stint as high-school
yearbook editor, in grade twelve, and a burgeoning interest in
photography, fostered by her mother who bought her a good 35
mm camera, and you get a fairly well-rounded personality. By
the time she graduated from high school Kathy Lang was
writing, playing, and singing her own songs, was quite profi-
cient at a number of sports, had taken up photography, owned
and operated a motorcycle, charted her own course when it
came to fashion ("Her mother says her unique fashion sense
developed early; she wore patched leather pants, sunglasses,
and a headband when she was eleven . . ." [Gillmor 33]), and
drove three-ton grain trucks for farmers in the summer holidays
to earn money.

Now, at the age of seventeen and a graduate of Consort High
School, it was time for Kathy Lang to hit the road. In her case,
the direction was west, to the nearest centre for higher learning:
Red Deer College.

Becoming a Professional

In the fall of 1979, when she was turning eighteen, Kathy Lang
left home to study music and voice at Red Deer College.
Speaking of her decision to move on, she said, "I enjoyed
growing up in Consort. I'm really a small-town girl at heart. At
the same time, I always wanted to be a musician and I was
interested in cities. I was happy to be in Consort, but I wanted
to get moving on" (Gillmor 33).

So she, like thousands before her who packed up and headed

Editorial

Another year. For some of us, it is the completion of our "primary" education. The times we spent will simply remain, "the times we had."

It has been my pleasure and honour to help compile 1978-79's memories into this years book. I sincerely hope it will help you remember the times; some good, some not so good, that we shared together in Consort School.

My thanks to my fellow yearbook members and to Ms. Rumohr. A very special thanks to Brenda McAllister whose experience was there when I needed it.

Good Luck to my assistant editor Monica Deleff and to the following editors there on.

Love,

Kathy Lang

FIGURE 7

Kathy Lang in grade twelve, wearing a suit and tie and editing Consort School's yearbook, Memories.

FIGURE 8

Kathy Lang the grade twelve graduate, heading out into the world for a career in music.

out of the sticks, signed up for those things she thought would interest her and would most benefit her career. Because of her considerable abilities in sports, she also thought it only natural to sign up for a team or two once she got to the college. Like a fair percentage of those thousands before her, she was mostly disappointed by what she found.

Saturday Night magazine claims she was "restless and unhappy with the narrow academic requirements" she encountered at Red Deer College (Gillmor 33). *Alberta Report* quotes Lang on the subject and she gets somewhat more specific: "They oppressed our creativity. If it couldn't be written down, they wouldn't accept it. They just didn't get it" (Philip, Whyte, and Cohen 39). What "they" most likely didn't get was that Kathy Lang was a special case, or at least someone who saw herself as a special case. The tolerance for eccentrics she found in her hometown was not so easy to find in a college setting.

People may drive tractors to school in a small town, but in a place like Red Deer it slows up traffic and creates a hazard, so the police step in and stop that sort of activity. Kathy Lang didn't want to toe the line the Red Deer College people had drawn across the classroom floor, or, for that matter, the one its athletic department had drawn around its volleyball courts, and when she didn't, they didn't go out of their way to accommodate her. In fact, as one friend remembers, they got downright antagonistic. Which isn't to say she didn't learn anything. The first thing she learned, whether she articulated it even to herself or not, was she was no longer a big fish in a small pond.

In Red Deer, having enjoyed success as a volleyball player in Consort, she tried out for the college team. She'd been a star in Consort, known to all the schools around, but, according to Kathy Naylor, her high school basketball coach, in Red Deer she received something of a comeuppance. The college coach could see he was dealing with talent and told Kathy she was the best player he'd seen from a small town, but he wouldn't have her on his team because of her attitude. Apparently the flamboyance that leads a player to sing on the court while wasn't something he was looking for on a college team. ays for Kathy this was a "real downer. She went to Red king she was good, and she was devastated."

Rather than be beaten, however, and run back home, as many have done in her situation, Lang took a completely different tack. She said when she left Consort she was always interested in cities, and she proved it. She headed for a bigger place — Edmonton — but not before she'd learned a thing or two about performance art.

Performance Art

She told Peter Gzowski on his CBC–TV show that she'd performed in garbage bags, "before garbage bags were in." She also did a thirty-six-foot "sky sculpture" with $500 worth of helium balloons, and in one marathon episode, took part in a twelve-hour reenactment of the famous Barney Clarke heart transplant in Utah, using a heart made of pickled vegetables.

These performances worked in well with her explorations of the avant-garde of music and art, with what she has described as "experimenting with noise" (Philip, Whyte, and Cohen 39), though they didn't win her any friends in the college administration. An old friend from those days, Wayne Gunnlaugson, recalls one incident in which Lang was going to put on her own concert "a jam session or some sort of thing" — and had put up posters advertising the event. Apparently, the dean came and tore them all down. "Mind you," says Gunnlaugson, "once she started to do well, Red Deer College was more than happy to take some credit, and that pissed her right off."

Life in Red Deer, though not within the confines of the college program, was, Lang claims, "sort of like being a beatnik. There was poetry reading and music 24 hours a day. I was living what I thought I had missed by missing the '60s" (Philip, Whyte, and Cohen 39). Gunnlaugson remembers there were lots of parties and lots of going out to the rock-and-roll and country bars in downtown Red Deer, as raw and brash a small city as one could hope to find.

He also remembers Lang had a particular fondness for old cars, and for the 1963 Mercury Monterey in particular, with its slanted, automatic back window. He recalls that he and a close friend of Lang's, Kelly Clarke, helped her find such a car and that they worked on it in Clarke's garage. Clarke, who still lives and works in Red Deer, was also a guitar player, and Gunnlaugson remembers his two friends playing frequently together and that Clarke helped Lang practise her material for school.

Another close friend of Lang's and her "constant companion and musical mentor" at Red Deer was a man named Gary Elgar (Philip, Whyte, and Cohen 39). Known to his friends as Drifter, he came west from Ontario to work on the oil rigs but ended up in the music program at Red Deer College. Lang claims he was "very much like John Lennon" and that she and Elgar were "the same person in different bodies, we were that close. Our relationship was very spiritual — it was also Platonic" (Philip, Whyte, and Cohen 39). Don Gillmor writes that the relationship was "cemented by a stated spiritual connection and a mutual interest in poetry, music, and hashish" (33). Judging from the vehemence of anti-drug statements Lang has made in the press since that time, the hashish was a temporary thing.

Lang had signed up for a two-year course in the music program, but left after a year and a half. However, the lack of a diploma to say she knew something about music has been anything but a handicap. When talking to an *Alberta Report* interviewer, in fact, Lang claimed to be proud of leaving without a diploma, adding with characteristic brash self-confidence, "considering I'm the best thing that's ever come out of there" (Philip, Whyte, and Cohen 39). It has become obvious that her encounter with the rigidity of a set music program and its requirements, her experimentation with various forms of music and sound and with the performance aspect of art, and her development of a strong friendship with a musical mentor, combined to strengthen her ambition to make a musical career for herself. Leaving the music program was an indication, most importantly to herself, that she would have this career on her own terms. And a student of music quitting a music program in order to pursue a music career certainly bespeaks resolution and an undeniably high level of self-confidence.

There have been many examples of artists before Lang who quit art school (and art here is used in its broadest sense) to learn about art. Of those many, however, we only hear the stories of the ones who made it (members of the Beatles and the Rolling Stones come immediately to mind), and they all exude a self-assurance which both marks them for some level of greatness and astounds the rest of us still resisting any temptation to quit our classes or our jobs and put our talent and our belief in it on the line.

In the spring of 1981 Kathy Lang probably saw a lot of Highway 2 between Red Deer and Edmonton. By this time she'd landed a job in a stereo and record store in Edmonton, just the sort of job a musician would take to put food on the table while trying to make it in her chosen field. And she was trying. An *Alberta Report* article claims she managed to record a jingle for a waterbed company, and the writer of the article, Tom Philip, recalls in that issue's publisher's note that he had first seen Lang in Red Deer while he was a reporter for the *Red Deer Advocate*. "I'd see her from time to time at parties where she'd play a guitar and sing this very off-the-wall stuff. I thought she was talented, but she was so weird it was hard to tell" ("*AR* This Week").

Whatever aesthetic impression she may have made on those around her, getting the attention of members of the local press was another way of helping her fledgling career. As many a wise soul in the entertainment business has said, all the talent in the world with no one to notice doesn't mean a thing.

She also got the attention of Edmonton country singer Holly Wright when Lang stopped her in a hotel parking lot and did an "impromptu audition" for the established singer (Philip, Whyte, and Cohen 39). Wright invited Lang to open for her at a concert at the Alberta Provincial Museum on 13 November 1981. It was Lang's first appearance in Edmonton.

Country Chorale

Her second appearance was thanks to another person who heard her singing and playing at a party in Red Deer. Doug Newell, who for that year was teaching in the Drama Department at

Red Deer College, was coproducing a play with Theatre Network, in Edmonton. The play was *Country Chorale*, a country musical with lyrics and dialogue by Ray Storey and music by John Roby, the same pair who had written two other musicals, *The Dreamland* and *Girls in the Gang*.

Country Chorale is the story of a young woman named Ruby who dreams of being a country singing star. She meets the boy of another part of those dreams, gets pregnant, which doesn't figure in the dream at all, and gets carted off to live and work on a quarter of land way back in the bush. Her only solace in this miserable existence is a radio program called *Country Chorale*.

In the production of this play, the lighting alternates between Ruby and four women standing off to the side. Each of the four women has a distinctive vocal style and they present the music Ruby hears on the radio. Together they embody Ruby's emotional state on stage. When Ruby is happy, the chorale sings an upbeat song, and when Ruby is sad, out come the weepers.

At the time Newell heard Lang in Red Deer, in the fall of 1981, Theatre Network artistic director Stephen Heatley was desperately searching for an actor to play the fourth member of the chorale, June Ritter. Storey and Heatley were looking for someone who could sing in a country style, with any luck like the late, great country star Patsy Cline. Newell heard Lang and immediately phoned Heatley, who then turned around and phoned Lang and offered her the job. He told her he couldn't give her any money, but she agreed anyway.

Nola Augustson, the actor who played Ruby, remembers that when Lang first showed up she had shoulder-length or longer hair, wore no makeup, and was very quiet. Because she had been called by the director and didn't have to audition and put herself on the line, and also probably because she'd never been in a professional theatrical setting before, Lang, as Augustson remembers her, remained withdrawn. Heatley says when she showed up she actually called herself a blues singer who "was into very atonal, dissonant stuff" and who didn't think she liked country music all that much.

The attitude that made Lang unwilling to fit herself into the structure of Red Deer College carried over into her initial involvement with Theatre Network. Heatley remembers that she didn't want to sing in the keys that John Roby had written, but this lack of enthusiasm probably had as much to do with an insecurity about the material as anything else. Lang didn't think she had much of a vocal range, but Roby wanted her to go higher than she was used to and, as Heatley remembers, he insisted she do so.

Augustson says Lang stayed on the edge of everything, including the play's production, "until one song, a ballad, struck her fancy, and she really decided to sing it rather than just go through it." Augustson can't remember exactly, but she's "pretty sure" the song was "Tears in My Eyes," and the way Lang sang it "really took everyone. Ray Storey was at the back of the hall, pacing, worried that his show was never going to get off the ground. When she started to sing, he started to dance. His play was going to work."

Introducing Patsy Cline

Heatley recalls Storey suggesting to Lang that she could get right into her part by fashioning her stance and musical style after those of Patsy Cline. Lang's reported response was, "Who's Patsy Cline?" — hardly unusual for someone born less than two years before the singer's death in 1963 and who claimed not to care very much for country music. In retrospect, however, Lang's response is very interesting, considering the later k.d. lang's studied involvement with the Cline legacy.

Country Chorale opened in March 1982 in Red Deer, where it played for two weeks, then moved to Edmonton for a similar run, all the while garnering good reviews. Heatley remembers that some of the reviews made particular mention of "a mysterious creature in the background," that creature being Kathy Lang.

She wore what Augustson describes as an aquamarine dress and blue earrings, and Heatley says that Nola had to help her do her hair and makeup because she'd never done it before. Lang thought it was all very funny that Nola would roll her hair. Indeed, Augustson recalls Lang had never even worn high heels before. None of these facts should count as strikes against a young woman born in the era of Germaine Greer, Gloria Steinem, and Betty Friedan, but they did seem odd to an actor like Augustson who, no matter what her personal convictions, was used to "being" whomever a role required, and dressing and making herself up accordingly. They are also somewhat amusingly inconsistent with the character of the person on whom Kathy Lang, and later, k.d. lang, modelled herself.

By the time of her death in an airplane crash on 5 March 1963, in Camden, Tennessee, Patsy Cline was at the top of her craft and profession as part of the new "Nashville Sound." This was the lush new sound orchestrated in so-called Music City, USA, by such architects as producer/guitarist Chet Atkins, vocal arranger Anita Kerr, and producers Owen Bradley (who would later produce Lang's *Shadowland*) and Don Law. The Nashville Sound was developed to counter the huge encroachments made on country's market by rock and roll. Country's hillbilly and redneck roughness was smoothed over, in the words of Robert K. Oermann in *The Country Music Book*, by "violin sections, soft background voices, sophisticated arrangements, and studio technology" (84).

Cline was made over in this image and looked the part of the glamorous new crossover star Nashville was trying to promote. She may have had humble beginnings and some fairly wild characters still in her life, notably her husband, but she dressed well, made herself up lavishly, drove a fine car, and lived in a beautiful house — everything the Nashville establishment wanted to project to the world as being a far cry from rough-and-tumble hillbillies.

That a rough-and-tumble singer like Kathy Lang, who wouldn't kowtow to the strictures of a music program and who was willing, initially, to take the same attitude with Theatre Network, would be convinced to model herself on the outwardly sophisticated and carefully groomed Patsy Cline is not just amusing, it also probably says a lot about Lang's attitude to a challenge. But, more of that later.

Stephen Heatley says that Kathy Lang proved to be "not a very good actress, but very watchable." Nola Augustson agrees and says that once Ray Storey had given her some advice on a good country singer stance, "she struck a pose and kept it. The intensity of that pose caught everyone's attention." Augustson goes on to amplify this by adding that Lang "always had enormous presence," and Heatley concurs. "She had incredible concentration. She could assume her character and stand and stare for a very long time."

Despite good reviews, Theatre Network's willingness to tour the show, and Lang's desire to stay with the company, she was not able to go on the road with *Country Chorale*. Augustson recalls that in order for the company to tour and stay financially afloat it had to cut back one actor. To do this it would fuse one of the radio singers with, what she calls, "a ditzy girl persona" from the regular cast. Lang wanted to keep singing in the show but couldn't stomach the idea of playing a "ditz," as well. So Lang was cut. Auguston says that Heatley still wonders about turning down the woman who would become k.d. lang, but she goes on adamantly to say that he turned down the actor, not the singer.

Augustson recalls two other things about her time with Kathy Lang. The first is that once *Country Chorale* opened, Lang's mother and one of her sisters came to the show and they "thought she was the greatest thing that ever happened." Augustson remarked warmly upon the obvious family support.

The second thing Auguston recalls is that after Lang had become part of the show she told the other members of the company that she always knew she'd be famous and that they all nodded their heads agreeably and said, "Yeah, yeah, sure." She then announced to the cast that "when she set off to be a star, she'd be known as *k.d. lang.*" When the time came, a new person would emerge.

The Invention of k.d. lang

When *Country Chorale* started to tour in the late fall of 1982, Kathy Lang was not along. But Nola Auguston recalls that by the time she got back to Edmonton in the summer of 1984 a singer named k.d. lang was setting the town afire and was scheduled to sing at the kick-off dance of the Edmonton Fringe Festival, an extravaganza of alternative and out-of-the-mainstream (sometimes way out) theatrical productions. Augustson claims, with a certain degree of pride, that from the start of the tour that almost included Kathy Lang to the time when people throughout Edmonton were familiar with k.d. lang and her band the reclines, "maybe a year" had elapsed.

Whether or not Augustson has all her dates right, what's clear is her amazement at her friend's rapid accomplishment of those things Lang spoke of doing during the original *Country Chorale* run.

Lang's rapid rise was given an early boost when she answered an Edmonton newspaper advertisement in May 1983 calling for a female country vocalist to sing in a Texas swing band. (Texas swing, also known as western swing, is a fusion of "country and western string bands with the horn arrangements of Dixieland and Big Band jazz" [Pareles and Romanowski 587].) The musicians who put out the call had booked studio time at Homestead Recorders Ltd., an Edmonton studio owned by Lars (or Larry) Wanagas, a man who also managed local bands. Wanagas told *Alberta Report* in 1984 about Lang's first visit to his studio: "[S]he didn't have her current act yet. She just sang some straightforward country songs, Emmy Lou [sic] Harris and Patsy Cline, but she sang them exceptionally well. It was obvious she had a lot of talent" (Philip, Whyte, and Cohen 41).

That first meeting between lang and Wanagas, which led to a management deal and a friendship that have lasted to this day, has become the stuff of country music legend — at least a Canadian one. *Canadian Musician*, in an April 1987 article, was wildly enthusiastic:

> The audition must have been spectacular. One witness to that fateful event remarked, "anyone who can sing that well lying on the studio floor or draped over the grand piano should be incredible standing up." Standing, sitting, writhing, or wiggling, Kathy Lang slayed Larry Wanagas then and there, and, as her manager now contends, "I haven't let her out of my sight since." (Stern, "Sustaining" 28)

Lang's unconventional studio demeanour would sound remarkably familiar to those who witnessed her antics on the high school basketball court or at parties in Red Deer. At Homestead Recorders it gave new witnesses something to talk and write about by adding that little extra oomph to a large amount of natural and energetically cultivated talent. It pushed Lang beyond the range of darned fine singers into that other realm where the singer becomes a personality, someone different, someone people want to notice.

Wanagas signed Lang to a management and publishing agreement in the summer of 1983 and then, as *Canadian Musician* puts it, "asked her what she wanted to do with her amazing voice" (Stern, "Sustaining" 29).

> When she first came to me, [Wanagas] recalls . . . she said she wanted to be a jazz singer. I said if you want to be a jazz singer the first thing to do is build yourself a little platform so that once you have some notoriety and success, you have a lot easier time with it. If we start pushing you as a jazz singer at 20 years old, we're all going to starve. If you want to do something off the wall . . . you'd better get a platform to work from. (Stern, "Sustaining" 29)

The article goes on to say that "[i]n relatively short order K.D. Lang (or k.d. lang, as she would have it) was born" (29).

This birth, or "unique creation" as *Canadian Composer* would, probably more accurately, have it (Flohil, "Voice" 6), has also become the stuff of country music legend. Indeed, thanks to the unflagging interest of both local and national media in the early stages of the k.d. lang phenomenon, the "unique creation" has become a widely known part of Canadian musical history and even something of a burden for the singer herself. But that's not the way she was thinking back in 1983.

Back then she needed people like Ray Storey to help her create a stage persona by giving her a stack of old Cline records to work on her country singer characterization. Lang gives the story a further push and a bit of a twist in a *Starweek* interview where she responds to the question of how she first connected with Patsy Cline:

It was a couple of simultaneous instances. My siblings, both my brother and my sister, told me to listen to Patsy Cline . . . I was playing a role in a musical . . . where I emulated a singer like Patsy Cline. So that started it. Then on my 21st birthday I got a bunch of Patsy Cline records and I started to listen. A couple of years before that I saw myself doing country but I didn't have the whole picture, it was like a couple of pieces were missing. I got out the Cline records and it just went click. . . . I saw myself, how I was going to dress, how I was going to move. I saw the kind of singing I was going to do, saw how my band was going to sound. (lang, "k.d. lang Interview" 12)

Once again, people's memories of events, and when those events occurred, don't necessarily coincide, but the important point here is that Lang's connection with Cline came about through a "couple of simultaneous instances."

Reincarnation

Another simultaneous instance gave the Cline connection a mystical aura, which in turn helped to inspire the name of Lang's band. *Alberta Report*, like many publications in the years 1983–85, made big on Lang's assertion that there was more to her fascination with Patsy Cline than the simple adoption of a sound or a style:

She began to recall a dimly remembered dream that recurred throughout her childhood; a plane, a storm outside, and a fiery crash. "All of a sudden, it just went click. The more I [Lang] believed it the more I felt it, and the more I felt free enough to believe it." (Philip 41)

What Lang remembered from her childhood dreams bore a remarkable resemblance to some of the details of the airplane crash that killed Patsy Cline a year-and-a-half after Lang was born. Part of what "just went click" was the idea that Lang, now k.d. lang, was the reincarnation of Patsy Cline, and so her band became the reclines — a fact, or a joke, that had to be explained many times over in the press.

And the press certainly had a field day with the whole reincarnation idea. Here was a subject from the realm of such unexplained phenomena as UFOs and various other forms of life after death, usually headlined only in the supermarket tabloids, but now fair game in the so-called respectable press because the person spouting all these wild ideas wasn't just some kook, she was a local and highly talented kook.

A notice in the 5 December 1983 *Alberta Report* said, ". . . Miss Lang insists she's the re-incarnation of celebrated U.S. singer Patsy Cline . . ." (Dolphin), but by 12 October 1984 the music critic in the Vancouver *Province* was careful with the reincarnation theme and said, "It's been noted, many times, that she believes the late Patsy Cline lives on in her soul" (Harrison). lang's reported response came as a correction to the writer, who felt she was "leery of sounding like a Rocky Mountain mystic." Said lang of Cline: "She comes through me" (Harrison). By the time lang made it across the country to Toronto to appear at clubs there, she was getting somewhat testy about the Cline uproar she had started. She told a *Toronto Star* interviewer on 1 November 1984,

I *am* a reincarnation of Patsy Cline. . . . I'm not tired of talking about it — but I am tired of people thinking it's a put-on. Somehow I've inherited her emotions, her soul. I know that sounds weird, but I *do* believe it. I have a recurring dream about a plane crash . . . and others where I actually have conversations with her. (Quill)

On the same day as the *Toronto Star* interview appeared, an article in the *Globe and Mail* quoted lang as saying she did claim "a real sense of psychic connection to Patsy Cline," but she quickly put the hype in "perspective" by adding, "[I]f some idiotic interviewer asks me if I'm *really* the reincarnation of Patsy Cline, of course I'm going to say yes" (Lacey).

A later *Maclean's* article (13 May 1985) stated simply that lang's modelling herself on Cline for her role in *Country*

Chorale "inspired her to develop her own musical identity." Said lang, "When I heard Patsy I heard jazz, rockabilly and blues all incorporated into country music. It was like she came knocking at my door and I acknowledged her" (Hayes).

Theatre Network's Stephen Heatley remembers Kathy Lang as a blues singer. Larry Wanagas claims she first told him she wanted to sing jazz. While living in Consort, lang says she listened to a lot of rock and roll. From what she said in *Maclean's*, it looks as if she found all those things in the music of Patsy Cline. Kathy Lang of Consort, Alberta, was meant to be the singer and entertainer k.d. lang, but between the two, she needed to be Patsy Cline, or at least some parts of her, for a while.

One way in which this new invention of Kathy Lang's, this k.d. lang character, was distinctly not like Patsy Cline was in her manner of dress, at least stage dress. The description of lang in concert that opens this book is a fair representation of how she chose to present herself to the public. As a brief refresher, here's the way Liam Lacey described her in the fall of 1984 in the *Globe and Mail*: "No standard-issue country cutie, K.D. sports a punk haircut, old-fashioned metal-frame glasses and cut-off cowboy boots with work socks rolled down around her ankles." One notices immediately that Lacey starts with a negative — he tells his readers what lang *isn't*, because at the beginning of her career, when she was starting to be noticed by the press, to call her a country singer, a *female* country singer, that is, and to include a description of her appearance, required some qualification by the writer.

The Female Country Look

At one time everyone knew what female country singers, or "girl singers," as they were often called, looked like because of an almost indelible impression made upon the general consciousness by the women stars of the Nashville Sound era. In the late fifties and the sixties, women like Patsy Cline, Tammy Wynette, Loretta Lynn, and Dolly Parton were all heavily made

FIGURE 9

*This was the k.d. lang who crisscrossed Canada
in 1984 and set the country ablaze.*

up, wore glittery, expensive gowns, and often had their hair piled up high on their heads in curls and ringlets, like a bouffant beacon or some variation of a queen's crown. And these *were* the queens of country music.

Prior to this era, women singers like the early Kitty Wells and Rose Maddox dressed like Roy Rogers's wife, Dale Evans, in shiny blouses with pearl snap buttons and full skirts occasionally decorated with rhinestones, or in fringed buckskin blouses and skirts. These were the female counterparts of men like Rogers and Gene Autrey who had made it big in Hollywood westerns, a wildly popular phenomenon. This was the era (the thirties and forties) during which country music became known as country and western music. Following this era, when cowboy movies lost their influence and Nashville tried to clean up its image and internationalize itself, country music readily dropped the "western" part of the name, though it hangs on in some quarters.

Following the time of the Nashville Sound, in the country-rock and country-pop era, women like Crystal Gayle (Loretta Lynn's younger sister), Emmylou Harris, and Linda Ronstadt all let their hair down considerably (in Crystal Gayle's case, down almost to her feet). However, whether they wore buckskin or silk, Girl Guide uniforms or cowboy boots, it didn't take the audience, particularly the men, very long to figure out these were indeed women.

k.d. lang went against, or at least thoroughly mixed up, the traditions of dress adhered to by previous generations of female country singers. The one she rejected most obviously was that of the reigning "country queens," Wynette, Lynn, and Parton. (Though to be fair, they have drastically toned down, and even gone against, that sixties image.) lang took some of the forties cowgirl look, married it to a palatable version of England's Sex Pistols look, and behold — country punk, another label lang doesn't like.

Another way in which the k.d. lang invention was not a full reincarnation of Patsy Cline was her manner on stage. The way she conducted herself at Homestead Recorders at her first audition was only a hint of what was to come. Here was a great bundle of energy that had to break loose: a young woman who refused to be held captive by a single spotlight trained on a microphone, as so many "girl singers" before her had been. The *Toronto Star* called her "a dervish, a shivering bag of antics" (Quill), and the *Globe and Mail* reported that she was "a mad, frenetic performer who runs about the stage, into washrooms and out doorways as she sings" (Lacey).

Here was something totally new on the Canadian, or any, music scene: a wild and crazy woman who dressed and cut her hair sort of like a man; who even tried, it seemed, to make herself look unattractive; but who had an immense amount of readily recognizable talent. With that previously unheard of combination she was assailing the hallowed halls of country music, a bastion of painful contradictions most noted for its supposed rigidity of divisions between Christian and secular, country and pop (or rock), and certainly, male and female.

The Country Humour Tradition

One should pause here and note, however, for the sake of accuracy, that lang was not the first person in country music to make a fool of herself on purpose, or even purposefully make herself look unattractive and even stupid. One of lang's heroes and a person who, in turn, admires lang, is Minnie Pearl. She has been playing the part of the country hick for years and is revered for her act and for her personality.

Going way back to the thirties, before Nashville decided to clean the ridge-runners and hayseeds off its streets and put them all in suits (a move imitated by the CBC in 1969 when it cancelled *Don Messer's Jubilee*), Roy Acuff, now a pillar of the country music establishment, was recording sides with a band called the Crazy Tennesseeans. (He later changed the name to the Smoky Mountain Boys to make it more respectable.) Two members of his band, Pete "Brother Oswald" Kirby and Rachel Veach (not a Smoky Mountain *Boy*), used to dress up as country rubes and play tunes such as "Weary Lonesome Blues" as comic pieces for big laughs. Surviving pictures of this pair, who were likely the ultimate caricature of dumb country hicks, must have given the architects of the Nashville Sound the shivers.

Two things about such rubes and hay-shakers as Kirby and Veach, though, are that they were both very talented musicians, and, no matter how lost in the backwoods or the bargain table of the Five and Dime they tried to look, they maintained a strict line between what was male and what was female. lang had all the former things going for her, but she added a new tint to an old picture by adopting what the press would come to call an "androgynous" look.

All these aspects of this new invention, this "k.d. lang," came together to answer a question that initially plagued manager Larry Wanagas. Here's how *Canadian Musician* put it:

> Both Kathy and Larry knew that what she had in the way of a voice was dynamite. She could coo, she could croon, she could holler and she could rock. The voice was in the bag, but what about the package? Once again Lang's spontaneous combustion answered the question; she would be nuts, wacky, or in her terms, she would have an "edge." (Stern "Sustaining" 29)

Now lang was ready to go out and take on the world.

Taking on the World

Once Larry Wanagas signed k.d. lang to a management agreement in the summer of 1983 — the western swing band having fallen apart after one gig — he assembled some studio musicians to make a demonstration tape. The money for this project came partly from lang, who had borrowed it from her mother, and partly from Wanagas, in the form of donated studio time.

Out of these sessions, eventually (spring 1984), came lang's first single, "Friday Dance Promenade," a sashaying honky-tonker, complete with a tip of the cowgirl hat to Patsy Cline, and all dressed up for country radio format. On the B-side of the record was "Damned Old Dog" by Maggie Roche, one of the New York Roche sisters. The song has been described as being "so perversely weepy a country ballad it walks a line between perfection and parody" (Zimm), so the pair of songs allowed lang to walk a familiar fence. An interesting sidenote here is that the Roche sisters sing a mix of urban folk, feminist, and what some critics have called "offbeat" bohemian material, and onstage, at least in the early eighties, they loved to camp up their performances by wearing loopy secondhand clothes and sporting duds. The similarities to lang's musical and fashion style are easy to see.

lang's studio band included ace session guitarist Amos Garrett (*Amosbehavin'*), a man who works the clubs from coast to coast and is probably still best known for his fluid lead guitar lines on Maria Muldaur's 1974 hit, "Midnight at the Oasis." The product of the sessions, a seven-inch single, was, according to the *Canadian Composer*, pressed on white vinyl and is now "an impossible-to-find collector's item" (Flohil, "Voice" 6).

This is another period in lang's life that's somewhat cloudy, with conflicting reports in the printed media. Even Wanagas has a hard time remembering the exact order in which events took place. However, his recollection is that once the single was recorded, the rhythm section of John Gray on bass and Jacek Kochan on drums stayed on while the rest of the studio musicians disbanded. To this duo was added Gordie Matthews on guitar and Stewart MacDougall on keyboards. This foursome headed out into the club world to play the first gig Wanagas was lining up.

In November, Wanagas went to work on Geoffrey Lambert, the general manager of Edmonton's Sidetrack Café, a club where such acts as Long John Baldry and Jesse Winchester plied their trade while in town. Lambert, as chronicled by *Alberta Report*, was sceptical, but he agreed to take a chance. "I guess I showed a lot of faith in Larry Wanagas," says Lambert. "I wasn't really sure when [lang] first came in here if I'd done the right thing. She looked kind of punkish, not really our type." As the *Alberta Report* article goes on to say, Lambert need not have worried: "She blew them all away. The dance floor was almost always packed, and when it wasn't K.D. was on it herself" (Philip, Whyte, and Cohen 41). The reviews of the show were good and, as lang herself says of it, "The talk had started" (Philip, Whyte, and Cohen 41).

Following the Sidetrack engagement, according to Wanagas, he and lang dropped the rhythm section and added Dave Bjarnason and Farley Scott, on drums and bass, respectively. This was now the lineup of k.d. lang and the reclines.

The talk lang spoke of got her booked beyond Edmonton, into such Calgary clubs as The Longhorn and into an appearance on the national TV show *Sun Country*. Just like Sidetrack manager Lambert, the folks on *Sun Country* weren't too sure about lang's appearance. And after all, this was a national "country" show. With that hair and those boots, was lang really country? Recalls lang in an *Alberta Report* notice, "First my cowboy boots were condemned. Then they came at me with a curling iron — they said they wanted to take the 'edge' off my hair" (Dolphin). But she did tone down her appearance for the show, and explained her rationale with a line that could easily stand as her basic philosophy of getting along with and within the entertainment industry: "I'll be anything they want me to be. . . . But then I'll turn around and be a thousand other things besides" (Dolphin).

Despite the fact that she chose to be herself and not what the country music establishment, wherever and however it exists, wished her to be, she gained an ardent fan in a later *Sun Country* host, Ian Tyson. Tyson, well known for such albums as *Old Corrals and Sagebrush* and the revered *Cowboyography*, plus such classic songs as "Summer Wages" and "Four Strong Winds," could see that, however lang was dressed, she had energy and immense talent. The *Canadian Composer* noted that at one Calgary club, where the audience sat mystified by lang's appearance and performance, Tyson shouted at them, "Why don't you people *dance*, . . . this band's fantastic" (qtd. in Flohil, "Voice" 6).

And so it went from the late fall of 1983 through the winter and into the spring of 1984, with lang touring the clubs and campuses of western Canada, and winning converts most places she went. In April 1984 lang was set to play one of these typical engagements at the Marmot Basin in Jasper, Alberta, when she got the news that her old friend and musical and philosophical mentor, Drifter, was dead. Apparently, according to an early article in *Alberta Report*, Gary Elgar had suffered a "massive brain haemorrhage after being assaulted at a party in

FIGURE 10

lang's backup band, the reclines, take a break. From left, Farley
Scott, Gordie Matthews, Stewart MacDougall, Dave Bjarnason.

Red Deer the night before" (Philip, Whyte, and Cohen 41). Later reports stated that he had tried to stop a fight at a party by stepping between the combatants, was punched, fell backwards, and hit his head. lang first heard the news five minutes before she was scheduled to go on stage.

"I got up there and sang my guts out," she told *Alberta Report*. "I couldn't understand why he'd been murdered. My spiritual side was always awake, but since Drifter's death it has been strong. He helped me. My music career has moved faster than any I can think of, and it's Drifter and Patsy who are doing it" (Philip, Whyte, and Cohen 41).

A Truly Western Experience

Later that same month, lang and her band headed for Homestead Recorders to record her first album, *a truly western experience*, in order to capitalize on gains she'd made on the road and to keep the momentum going. The *Canadian Composer* notes that despite the availability of a studio, "money was not in great supply," and the result was a "$5,000 effort that gives little idea of the power of the singer's voice, or the breadth of her material" (Flohil, "Voice" 6).

The part about the lack of funds is certainly true, and the observation that the album doesn't do justice to lang's talent and potential is probably also a fair assessment, especially considering the assessment is made by a magazine that concentrates on the Canadian musical scene from the specific angle of those who write the music. For the rest of the population, *a truly western experience* was a sit-up-and-take-notice kind of album — the official birth announcement, so to speak.

The cover, designed by lang, features a cut-and-paste farm scene in which lang walks a fence to a barn, in the loft of which is a picture of Patsy Cline. On the back is a construction paper hay wagon carrying lang's band, each member consisting of the appropriate construction paper musical instrument topped by a zany photo from a shopping mall take-your-own-photo box. Two construction paper legs and an arm protrude from a pile of paper hay, where the singer has obviously taken a dive. Along the bottom of the back cover, below the song titles and credits, runs the line "and the wind drifts through my soul, say hi to patsy for me," homage to two of lang's spiritual influences.

On the vinyl inside are nine songs, five of them written by lang and her band. Side one opens with an old fire-eating rockabilly number called "Bopalena," penned by Nashville stalwarts Webb Pierce and Mel Tillis. If this is a country album, then this song is the rooster crowing loudly and proudly in the barnyard. Next comes a Cline-like song written by lang called "Pine and Stew," where she slows down the pace and really does what many, many critics have said she does best, throws her whole self into a ballad. This is the cut that Peter Gzowski played regularly on his CBC *Morningside* program and called "the quintessential Canadian country tune" (Flohil, "Voice" 10). Then come the up-tempo and happy "Up to Me," written by keyboardist Stewart MacDougall, and "Tickled Pink," another mover, written by lang and the band, to round out side one.

"Hanky Panky," by lang and Gordie Matthews, gives side two a rousing and romping opening, and that's followed by the old E. Miller, D. Haddock, and W.S. Stevenson composition "There You Go," a Cline number done at a moderate waltz tempo. "Busy Being Blue," written by MacDougall, is next, and then a rollicking western swing number credited to Patsy Cline herself, "Stop, Look and Listen." (On the Patsy Cline reissue album *Stop, Look and Listen*, MCA 1440, this song is credited to C.C. Beam, C.L. Jiles, and L.B. Watts.)

The final tune on the album is one called "Hooked on Junk," a song about at least two kinds of junk, trash and heroin, written by Drifter and sung (sometimes spoken) and played by lang in a slow, at times rhythmically collapsing, and starkly introspective style. Reviewers have compared it to the compositions of Laurie Anderson, and it is also somewhat reminiscent of the experimental work John Lennon and Yoko Ono were doing in 1969 on the album *Unfinished Music No. 2: Life with the Lions*. The *Canadian Composer* calls the song "a reminder of her days as a solo performance artist" (Flohil, "Voice" 6), while lang herself told *Alberta Report* simply, "It's for Drifter. He wrote it. That's why I put it on the record" (Philip, Whyte, and Cohen 41).

The cover art on *a truly western experience* alone gives testimony to the facts that the album was done on the cheap; that it owes a little something to the punk influence on album cover art, which caught up even nonpunks like Linda Ronstadt (*Mad Love*) and the Rolling Stones (*Love You Live*); and that the artist, and her band, had a quirky sense of humour and, consequently, didn't take themselves too seriously.

Any experienced record producer would immediately judge the album to have a very weak centre, if any, and note that it wanders all over the place, trying, it would seem, to hit every musical style that ever influenced lang.

The inclusion of "Hooked on Junk" was a bold, some would say commercially suicidal, move. John Lennon, despite his stature, bombed with *Unfinished Music No. 2: Life with the Lions*. That lang chose to do her old friend's song, as a tribute to him, spoke well of her as a caring human being, and, in terms of her career, declared once again that she would do things her own way. There is much evidence in the press and in the testaments of people she's known and worked with along the way to suggest that lang works very hard to combine the caring and the career.

The album, by what many in the lang camp still consider a miracle, came out a day before she was to appear at the Edmonton Folk Festival in August 1984. That timing, together with a marvellous coincidence at the festival, were like a large gift. lang was scheduled to play for twenty-five minutes, but the act that was to follow her showed up late. This enabled her to stretch her act to forty-five minutes, and, in the words of Toronto publicist Richard Flohil, she "blew everybody else off the stage" (Hayes).

Here's the way Flohil remembers it:

Wearing her cutoff cowboy boots, a cream-colored suit circa 1955, and wing-shaped glasses (without lenses), Lang tore through her repertoire, winding up by responding to a standing ovation with an a cappella version of *Amazing Grace* which segued into *I'm Saved*, an old R&B standby which had been written by Leiber and Stoller for Lavern Baker back in 1960. As Lang stormed around the stage banging a parade marshall's bass drum, the crowd gave her another standing ovation. ("Voice" 6–8)

Flohil, as chronicled by *Alberta Report*, could barely contain his enthusiasm: "She was the best thing that happened all weekend. She had 10 times more energy than anyone else who hit the stage and her act was unlike anything I'd ever seen" (Philip, Whyte, and Cohen 43). Flohil beat a hasty retreat to his home base in Toronto in order to spread the word. He went immediately to the Brunswick House to book lang and found he had to take a number. "Some of Sylvia Tyson's musicians — Sylvia had been at the festival — had already been in there talking about [lang]" (Philip, Whyte, and Cohen 43).

lang Hits Toronto

Within a very few days lang was engaged to play for a week (29 October–3 November) at Albert's Hall, something of a blues bar in Toronto's Brunswick House, and this was just one part of a cross-Canada tour sponsored by the Edmonton Folk Festival (Quill). Flohil was delighted by Toronto's reception: "There was a line-up on a Monday night. . . . I don't think I've ever seen a line-up on a Monday in Toronto. She got incredible attention there. She was everywhere: in the *Globe*, on CBC radio, in the *Star*. She was so busy she turned down *Canada AM*" (Philip, Whyte, and Cohen 43).

Forget what Humphrey Bogart says of gold in *The Maltese Falcon*; media attention is the stuff that dreams are made of — at least in the music business. On the strength of her rousing performance at the Edmonton Folk Festival, and with an album in hand, lang didn't have to go looking for work and some notice in one of the big eastern cities — it came looking for her.

And what a darling of the media she turned out to be: that voice, those performances, her range of material, her confidence, her wit and desire, and then, like huge gobs of icing on the cake for all journalists eager to sell stories, her lowercase initials, her zany appearance, and, wonderfully, the whole Patsy Cline reincarnation business. For every newspaper entertainment writer weary of sitting long into many nights listening to the supposed next big thing, lang was fresh, original, exciting, and don't forget, "offbeat."

A *Maclean's* article suggested that "Lang has undeniable appeal to fans of country music, but her strongest support is from an urban audience searching for new trends" (Hayes). The same article cited Sylvia Tyson, famous folk singer and writer of the classic "You Were on My Mind," who enlarged on the above statement: "She can also be the darling of the avant-garde because she is so dynamic." And having found her, these new audiences were enthralled. lang was assertive and lang was fun, and she mixed these together with great Tabasco-like dashes of irony — the beating she took in her performance of "Johnny Get Angry," the mane of hair, and the strutting through "These Boots Are Made for Walking" — and irony was *the* intellectual currency of the eighties. With her performances and the media egging each other on, you practically had to be in a coma, at least in Canada, not to have heard of lang by the end of 1984, mid-1985 tops. No doubt about it, lang's brand of country had captured a wide audience not used to turning its attention to country music.

Like fans who found such blues masters as Robert Johnson and Muddy Waters through the music of the Rolling Stones, Eric Clapton, and Led Zeppelin in the late sixties, there can be little doubt that those who rediscovered Patsy Cline in the eighties owe a great deal to k.d. lang. Once people heard lang's versions of old Cline hits and heard her endorsing them enthusiastically (after reincarnation, how much more enthusiastic can you get?), listeners wanted to hear the originals. I have talked to happy owners of Patsy Cline records in cities like Edmonton, Saskatoon, Winnipeg, Toronto, and London, Ontario, who bought their records because of k.d. lang.

Reservations about lang

Despite such enthusiasm, however, both from lang and for her, not everyone was ready to throw aside their old allegiances and follow this new phenomenon. Soon after she broke big in Toronto, then in Montréal, Ottawa, Quebec, and Halifax, an article in *Alberta Report* stated that ". . . some industry observers doubt that her current act, her broad musical range and uniqueness are to her best advantage" (Philip, Whyte, and Cohen 43). The article went on to say that her "failure to appeal to a specific market has resulted in a minimum of air play" (44). A musical director for a country station in Edmonton spelled out early what many in the country music industry would hold against lang: "We're trying to play straight, contemporary country. K.D. Lang is a little too borderline. There are five cuts on her album that could potentially be played as country, but her image is as a rock singer" (Philip, Whyte, and Cohen 44).

Call it narrow thinking, prejudice, fear, or good business sense, this type of categorization swings both ways. *Alberta Report* quotes the musical director of another station as saying, "We're a top-40 radio station. She doesn't really fit our stuff. She has more of a country sound and we try to stay away from that unless we get a lot of requests for something" (Philip, Whyte, and Cohen 44). An article in the *Canadian Composer* echoed these words when it said one record company executive was "intrigued by [lang's] act and the performance, but worried that it might fall into the gulf he perceived existed between rock and country" (Flohil, "Voice" 8).

Unfortunately, this is the way many people think and how the music industry, in turn, responds. Or it's the way the music industry does business and forces its audiences to respond. People are somehow deemed incapable of taking in two or three types of music in rapid succession and enjoying them all, whether they wear cowboy hats or eight earrings, despite the fact that many of them grow up going to dances where the band will mix up rock, contemporary and old-time country, blues, and maybe even some eastern European tunes, and have the crowd howling for more. lang grew up with these kinds of get-togethers and she's not the first to face the unfortunate stigma of the musical establishment finding her hard to categorize and thus denying her a break.

It's a dog-eat-dog world and k.d. lang, a vegetarian, came along with the idea that she could be a lot of different things to a lot of different people. So did her manager. "We don't want to alienate anyone," said Larry Wanagas. "You can go to a K.D. Lang concert and see everyone from the weird-haircut alternative crowd to senior citizens. We want to keep it that way; it's best in the long run" (Philip, Whyte, and Cohen 43). But the long run was just getting started, and Nashville, self-proclaimed home of country music, would have its own ideas about who fit the country mould.

Before she could get anyone in Nashville to raise an eyebrow, however, lang had to attract the interest of the big record companies, most of which have their headquarters in the U.S. According to the *Canadian Composer*, Wanagas wanted a showcase date for lang south of the border but found that record executives there had no idea where Edmonton was. "I mentioned Wayne Gretzky to them," Wanagas recalls. "They'd never heard of him, either" (Flohil, "Voice" 8).

lang at the Bottom Line

But a deal came through to book lang into New York's famous Bottom Line nightclub in May 1985 on a bill with two other unknown bands. Thanks to a mention by Murray McLauchlan's manager, Bernie Finkelstein, to a *Rolling Stone* reporter, lang got a three-quarter page colour picture and blurb in the magazine's 20 June 1985 issue. Said the institution of rock and roll journalism: "At a showcase at New York's Bottom Line, she turned in a kinetic performance, do-si-do-ing primly around the stage at one moment and bellowing into the mike with the rage of Johnny Rotten the next. . . . Lang showed that she really can sing. Now, if only the Bobs and Bettys at the American record companies would take notice . . ." ("Canadian Cowpunk").

Going by what an *Alberta Report* article claimed immediately following lang's American debut, the executives certainly took notice. Columbia Records's Stephen Ralbovsky
responded, "She has that sort of special charm that captures
you involuntarily. I was captivated the whole time" (Elash).
However, the executives were not pulling out their pens to fix
a deal. That would come after lang's second visit to New York.

Between the two, lang returned to Toronto to play a folk
festival, a country music picnic, and Canada Day celebrations
at Harbourfront. "Within two weeks," says the *Canadian Composer*, "Lang had played for more than 25,000 people in the city"
(Flohil, "Voice" 8). Back at the Bottom Line, lang opened for
Boston's NRBQ (New Rhythm and Blues Quintet) and gave
another earth-shaker of a performance. This time someone
wanted to do business and that someone was Seymour Stein.

Stein, the founder of Sire Records and signer of Talking Heads,
Madonna, the Pretenders, and the Ramones, approached lang
and they talked about a singer as different from the just-
mentioned four acts as one could likely find, Canadian country
legend Wilf Carter. Having made contact, Stein made the pronouncement that has been quoted in many, many articles on
lang, and justifiably so: "You are what country music would
have been if Nashville hadn't screwed it up" (qtd. in Flohil,
"Voice" 8).

That did it. A deal was promised, and later signed on a boat
in Vancouver harbour, and it was agreed that a new album
would be recorded once a producer was found. lang headed for
Japan for a month in the summer of 1985 to play at Expo and
to film a documentary, *k.d. lang in Japan* (unreleased). But what
about that comment of Stein's that country music had been
screwed up by Nashville? And if so, how so?

Screwed Up by Nashville?

Many of the articles one can read on k.d. lang and her assault
on country music radio playlists like to see the evils of Nashville and its sway over an entire industry embodied in the

persona of Kenny Rogers. Rogers, singer of such hits as "The Gambler," "Lady," and "Don't Fall in Love with a Dreamer," is likely more a scapegoat for all those who have tried to make it in Nashville and didn't, than evil incarnate. But he does make a great target. He's got all his early rock and roll rough edges smoothed off, has a wholesome, teddy-bearish appeal, and makes millions of dollars singing songs so clean-sounding and well-produced that many complain they're overproduced and sound like they could have been made anywhere, not in the country music capital of the world.

Rogers, according to many people, is the final outcome of the Nashville Sound project that has now, also in the opinion of many, rendered the city an assembly-line hit factory, turning out one cloned product after another in studios manned by the likes of Billy Sherrill and Chips Moman.

As noted earlier, Nashville undertook this project in order to clean up its image and appeal to a wider range of listeners than it had previously. The cleanup seems to have been so total as to have stifled the creative urges of any artist who did not conform to the new Nashville code of making music. One person who wouldn't conform to the new regime was Waylon Jennings, a singer who once claimed he "couldn't go pop if he had a mouthful of firecrackers!" (qtd. in Riese 12).

Jennings went over the heads of the Nashville hierarchy and struck deals with the big New York label bosses on what material he would record and what musicians and producers he would record with. This action, which he undertook to maintain his creative independence, became the start of the so-called Outlaw movement of the mid-seventies, and he was joined by other artists such as Willie Nelson and Tompall Glaser.

At about the same time that Jennings was struggling for artistic freedom, the rest of Nashville was going through its own bout of soul-searching over the business — and it was big business — of crossover hits. These are songs that make it as hits on one chart — country, for instance — then cross over to another and hit big there. By doing so they appeal to a broad cross section of listeners, the kind lang and Wanagas both wanted, but not at the expense of compromising lang's integrity of vision or of watering down her attitude. By refusing to align herself with one group, and by hoping to appeal to many groups, lang didn't cross over, but fell through the cracks. Country crossover artists, on the other hand, ran the risk of alienating their first audience by aligning themselves with that group, then crossing over to another audience and appearing to have abandoned the first. The people who comprise the country audience are renowned for their intense loyalty, and they don't like being left behind.

Here's what writer Randall Riese, in his book *Nashville Babylon*, had to say about the reaction by some of the country music establishment to the aspirations of those who would appeal to a crossover audience:

> Country music stars are . . . encouraged to defend their genre of music with adamantine verve, to protect the purity of country music, and to profess the evils of rival pop (music) whenever possible. An amusing and symbolic illustration of this occurred in 1975 when Charlie Rich drunkenly stumbled onto the stage at the annual Country Music Association's awards show. Rich managed to articulate the nominated names for Entertainer of the Year award. However, when he saw the card with the name of the winner, John Denver, Rich took out his cigarette lighter and promptly set the offending card ablaze. For months afterward, Nashville simmered with scandal — not because of the public spectacle of the drunken star and the flammable name card, but rather because the Country Music Association had elected to bestow the most coveted award in country music to a *pop singer*! (12)

On the one hand, Nashville's "adamantine verve" in protecting the purity of its music is clearly in evidence, but on the other, Denver *did* get the award.

Whether or not Nashville's identity crisis can be explained as part of a general southern U.S. attitude that evolved under the burden of southern history is open to speculation. Does the South's checkered past give it an inferiority complex which shows up in its flip-flopping attitudes to what can and cannot be part of its indigenous music? There can be no doubt after an even cursory reading of the literature on southern history and musical genres that the South resents being told by the North (Nashville by New York, for instance, or even by Los Angeles) what it is that constitutes good music.

But the very fact there is such resentment indicates an insecurity about how the South is perceived by the rest of the U.S., and by the world. After southerner Jimmy Carter's meteoric rise to the presidency in the late seventies and his high-profile championing of such country stars as Loretta Lynn and Willie Nelson, his ignominious and very rapid fall from grace couldn't have helped the South's, and Nashville's, image either.

Rock music started in the same general geographic area as country music but rapidly developed many centres of influence, from Memphis to New York to London, England, and as a consequence could hardly have its image controlled by any "head office," as it were. Country music, on the other hand, despite excellent work coming out of such places as Austin, Texas; Bakersfield, California; and all of Canada, still manages to retain Nashville, Tennessee, as its focal point. (Contemporary Canadian country artists claim they can make a living in Canada without heading for Nashville, if they are content with a strictly Canadian market.) New country artists getting into the business, and lang was no exception, still talk about getting to Nashville. That's where Music Row is, the Grand Ole Opry, WSM radio — one of the first major voices of country music — the annual Country Music Association awards, and the annual Fan Fair. It's also where many, many country music stars have made their homes.

This is the place Seymour Stein was talking about. What he saw and heard in lang's performance at the Bottom Line was what he felt should have been the result of the natural progression of the best impulses in country music, all of which got lost in Nashville's desperate attempts to appeal to as many people as possible, and in the beatings it inflicted on itself for doing just that. lang's fiddle player and cowriter, Ben Mink, who used to play with FM, Cano, and Bruce Cockburn, and whom lang met in Japan at Expo '85, expanded on Stein's view of Nashville in *Canadian Musician*: "[T]hey diluted what was pure and honest about (country music) and it became a mishmash of all sorts of MOR [middle of the road] styles done badly" (Stern 31).

Angel with a Lariat

Back on the producer front, after courting at least three of them, Stein's people at Sire Records convinced roots-rockabilly song-writer/guitarist Dave Edmunds (who had a 1970 hit with a remake of Smiley Lewis's 1955 hit "I Hear You Knockin'") to produce lang's second album. However, he would only work in England, so recording of *Angel with a Lariat* would commence there in May 1986.

Meanwhile, back in Canada, lang won the Juno Award (an annual award celebrating excellence in the Canadian music industry) for the Most Promising Female Vocalist at the 4 November 1985 ceremonies in Toronto. lang used the occasion to create a sensation and add to her ever-growing catalogue of outrageous acts.

To accept her award she showed up in a traditional white wedding dress, complete with veil and white cowboy boots, and proceeded, in keeping with the category of her award, to *promise* (that age-old activity of brides, get it?!) to continue to sing for only the right reasons. While she later complained that most people hadn't understood the joke, and they hadn't, the press zeroed in on the visual impact and boosted lang's profile once again. The wedding dress image is, in fact, such a popular and enduring one that the CBC included it on its *Country Gold* television special, 1 and 2 February 1992.

Later in November, lang appeared back home in Edmonton to broadcast a coast-to-coast concert with the Edmonton Symphony Orchestra. Though some magazines called this an unlikely pairing, old rock fans will remember that the Edmonton Symphony backed up the English classical-rock band Procol Harum for its 1972 album, *Live in Concert.* lang's November concert with the orchestra also set the stage for a repeat performance in May at Expo '86 in Vancouver.

Following lang's appearance there, she and the reclines took

FIGURE 11

*lang attends the 1985 Juno Awards
ceremonies in a wedding dress.*

off for London to record at Maison Rouge studios with Edmunds. A July 1990 *Guitar Player* profile of the Welsh rocker said of him, "As a producer, he has become *the* man of choice for a dazzling roster of artists seeking the clean, uncluttered sound and gospel-like fervor that characterized '50s and early-'60s American music" (Sievert 43). During the era of Edmunds's interest, such musicians as Elvis Presley, Carl Perkins, Jerry Lee Lewis, and Johnny Cash were making rockabilly music (a frenetic hybrid of rock and country music) in Memphis and Nashville. For lang to go with Edmunds as her producer was to go back to the country music Stein was speaking of, "before Nashville screwed it up" — the kind of high-energy music lang had been presenting across Canada and with which she awakened interest in country music as she went.

The liner notes to *Angel with a Lariat* indicate that it was recorded from 26 May to 27 June 1986, and the April 1987 issue of *Canadian Musician* provides a fair glimpse of what went on in the studio. It's fair to say that the project was not made in heaven, but that lang and the reclines were all happy with the final product. The Canadians were not used to England and its lack of experience with country music. They also found that technically, in Ben Mink's words, the English "were far below our standards" (Stern, "Sustaining" 31).

For his part, Edmunds was aghast at lang's insistence on a hand-held microphone, feeling, most likely, that *England* was technically far beyond that. Mink describes lang's way of doing things: "When she sings she uses her whole body. When she goes for a low note she'll crouch over the same way she does on stage. She whips around — she's got fantastic mic[rophone] technique" (Stern, "Sustaining" 31). Fantastic or not, Edmunds had trouble with the lang project and told *Guitar Player*, "That one wasn't really up my street. There were things I didn't understand, like the polkas and weird stuff she does" (Sievert 50).

Said lang of the experience: "They [Sire] really wanted Edmunds and I just really wanted to record the album. I think one of the best things about it was that we were all on edge. Just the idea of being someplace new. London's a real music city, it has lots of history, and the edge of that came out in the studio" (Stern, "Sustaining" 31).

Angel with a Lariat does have an edge to it, a rocking, rollicking, big fun kind of edge to its basically country sound. Seven of its ten songs were written by lang, Mink, and other band members, who, on this project, included Gordie Matthews on guitar, Dennis Marcenko on bass, Ted Borowiecki on keyboards and accordion, Miche Pouliot on drums, Mink on violin, electric mandolin, and guitar, and lang on vocals.

The songs range from the drum-driven opener, "Turn Me Round," a spirited call to the dance floor, and one which is still a staple of Canadian country radio playlists, to the album's finale, "Three Cigarettes in an Ashtray," the gut-wrenching Cline torch ballad that lang had long been performing on stage to wild acclaim. (A dictionary definition of a torch ballad is "a sentimental song of unrequited love," as in carrying the torch for someone.) In between is "Diet of Strange Places," a honky-tonkin' piano song with a thumping bass and a lavish overlay of B.J. Cole's steel guitar that runs a lovely counterpoint to lang's lyrics of yearning: "Starving, I've got this hunger / growling, from deep within."

There is also the Cajun-sounding "Got the Bull By the Horns," with its frisky, *bon temps* accordion; the wild and joyfully atonal "Watch Your Step Polka," the idea for which lang has claimed came to her in a dream where newlyweds dance carefully around cow pies in a deserted gymnasium (Weiss B1); lang's technically more dramatic and easily more rocking version of the 1970 Lynn Anderson hit "Rose Garden" (which one source claims lang got the idea to do after hearing some drunks sing it on a London train [Caldwell and Geoffries]); and the album's title tune, a high-tempo country pickin' number with superb guitar drive, fills, and trills by Matthews and plenty of throaty, power vocals from lang.

Angel's cover features a 3-D illustration by Amy Vangsgard of ceramic horses flying past a colourful archway decorated with ceramic airplanes, guitars, trophies, monkey wrenches, ice skates — the list goes on — plus plenty of angels and cherubs. On a pedestal in the middle of the archway is a ceramic naked woman, and perched on her head is a Holstein cow. Flying through the midst of it, suspended between the horses by what could be a bullwhip or a curtain cord, is lang in a simple black dress, black tights, and her cutoff boots and work socks.

On the back is a black-and-white photo of lang in a western outfit, complete with big hat and fringed jacket, backstage at the Commodore, in Vancouver. On one side of the inner sleeve is another black-and-white photo, this one a head shot of a fairly serious looking lang, and on the other side is another serious study of lang, in which she wears a derby hat and stands before a large photo of a field of stooked wheat. In the field, the reclines, dressed in matching western outfits, dance with identical white cardboard cutouts of cowgirls.

lang Sheds Her Glasses

Once again, there's the quirky sense of humour, but gone is the spiky hair and, most significantly, gone are the rhinestone glasses. *Canadian Musician* called this move, besides the recording of the new album, "the biggest thing that's happened to Lang in '86" (Stern, "Sustaining" 30). The article went on to say that lang talked about the abandonment of her trademark "with the seriousness of an arms negotiator," and that the glasses represented the difference between Kathy and k.d.. A March 1987 article in *Alberta Report* celebrating *Angel's* release quoted lang saying much the same thing:

> The reason I've tempered my style . . . is because I'm taking my music more seriously. I'm tired of being written about as some zany, crazy kid. I think the gap between K.D. and Kathy has lessened to the point where I'm almost completely Kathy on stage now. (Caldwell and Geoffries)

The article went immediately on to say that this toning down of lang's country-punk image "might mollify country fans, who in the past have criticized the Albertan for parodying their staple music." Here was something lang likely hadn't reckoned on, that not only would her music not fit country playlists, but that she'd also be perceived as not being serious about country music — that she was making fun of it.

FIGURE 12

lang, the Angel with a Lariat.

Many articles, like one in the *Los Angeles Times*, carried titles that asked the big question: "Did Lang Come to Praise or Parody?" (Hilburn).

Praise or Parody?

The occasions for Americans to ask whether lang had come to praise or parody country music became more frequent when *Angel with a Lariat* was set for release in spring 1987 by an American company with international clout.

In September 1986 lang made her American television debut on *Late Night with David Letterman*, dressed in too-late-for-the-Salvation-Army style. Her appearance with Letterman prompted the folks at *Hee Haw*, the country musical-comedy program from Nashville, to invite lang to do a couple of songs on their show. They were favourably enough impressed with her performance that two songs became four and she recorded two shows instead of the one.

Angel was released in March 1987 and to support it lang went on a Canada/U.S. tour from March to August. The Canadian reviews of the album were generally enthusiastic while the Americans were more guarded. *Rolling Stone* said she was "all over the place" and that her band "isn't yet supple enough to make her thematic changes sound of a piece" (Guterman, rev. of *Angel* 136), which was much in the vein of the negative remarks made about the scattered quality of the first album. The magazine did, however, point out that when lang turned her voice loose on midtempo numbers such as "Three Cigarettes in an Ashtray" and "Diet of Strange Places," she entered "honky-tonk heaven" and "makes most of today's neo-traditional country kids sound Hollywood" (Guterman, rev. of *Angel* 136, 139).

Whatever they said about the album, the Americans had mostly praise for her live shows. The *Los Angeles Herald Examiner* titled its review of her performance at the Roxy in L.A., "Lang Carries a Torch for Country," and claimed in its

FIGURE 13

*The folks on the David Letterman show asked lang if
she was going on with those holes in her stockings.*

subtitle, "Roxy Rolls with Singer's Manic Intensity" (Weiss).
Variety magazine said of the same show,

> Radiating confidence, charm and cheer, Lang was pro-
> fessional but not slick, virtuoso but not a showoff. Her
> compelling intensity and fresh good looks riveted attention
> as she belted, growled, keened and delivered the blues full
> voice, astonishing both technically and stylistically.
> (Zimm)

Despite such enthusiasm, there were still reservations about lang's commitment to country music. *Variety*, for instance, though it loved her performance and got a great kick out of the humour she wrung from "Johnny Get Angry," "Damned Old Dog," and "Rose Garden," called attention to its observation that the "minute distance between this Canadian country-come-lately and her adopted genre appeared at wry moments" (Zimm). In other words, lang walked a thin line between praise and parody, leaving the audience to ask, Was she having fun at the expense of country music?

In response, lang told *Maclean's* that she was "having fun with country, not at the expense of it" (Jennings and Bell 50), and that her toned-down image gave evidence of that fact. *Maclean's* even linked this toning down to the public's increasing respect for country music in general in the mid- to late-eighties. Putting this statement in the context of lang's career, the magazine asserted that lang "helped pioneer country's new chic by bringing it in the back door of high camp" (Jennings and Bell 50).

Now that she was being noticed by members of the American country music establishment, her shift in image included such onstage costumes as a blue-sequined evening gown and long white gloves, dress with which Patsy Cline would have been familiar. "Change is the essence of growth," claimed lang. "You must take a look at where you came from, but keep moving ahead" (Jennings and Bell 50).

Also to the question of whether, as the *Los Angeles Times* put it, "her eccentric approach is more studied or soulful," lang replied,

I think performance art plays a big role in what I do on stage, especially humor. I think there is a lot of humor in country music. It's just that it has been forgotten. Go back 20 years and you find a lot of humor in people like June Carter, Minnie Pearl, Grandpa Jones and Rose Maddox. There was a great openness and spirit in them.

At the same time, what I'm doing wouldn't work if it wasn't coming from my soul. It's not just some intellectual process. I love country music. . . . I grew up listening to that music and it is a part of me . . . part of my background. (Hilburn)

Though lang perhaps couldn't make the self-righteous claims Barbara Mandrell does in her hit song "I Was Country When Country Wasn't Cool," her statement to the *Times* was essentially true.

A *Canadian Musician* article noted that while many Canadians who initially flocked to lang's musical style and dress might be put off by her new image, thinking she had lost her "edge" in order to cater to the American market, the Americans still thought she was plenty weird. Plenty weird or not weird enough, lang maintained a level of confidence bordering on outright boldness. She told *Canadian Musician* quite matter-of-factly, "I'm going to change country music," then put herself in the context of the development of the genre:

Let's say Hank Williams was the first generation. Then you have people like Gram Parsons and Emmylou Harris. Then you have people like Rank and File and Jason and the Scorchers. And then you have people like Dwight Yoakam and k.d. lang. (Stern, "Sustaining" 30)

In the same vein she told *Alberta Report* that her "personal goal is to understand the business enough to manipulate the rules" (Caldwell and Geoffries). Whether or not Nashville would allow her to achieve that goal, or whether, as *Maclean's* noted of country music in general, its overall change would make it easier for Nashville to accommodate lang's ambition, was yet to be seen. She did, however, appreciate the challenge of taking on an artistic genre that had strict boundaries. She told *Canadian Musician*, "That's why I chose country music. It has such a structure that I find the potential to challenge it really exciting" (Stern, "Sustaining" 30).

The "Girl Singer" Tradition

Besides the structure of the musical form itself, lang would also have been familiar with the structure that the country singer's — and particularly the female country singer's — life is supposed to have. The stories by now are legion of how Loretta Lynn, Dolly Parton, and Tammy Wynette, early in their careers, were chained to gruelling schedules designed by men and how, in order to save themselves, they eventually had to fight their way out of those schedules and that dominance.

A 1977 *Rolling Stone* article described Loretta Lynn being knocked about by fans and chased to her tour bus and back to the auditorium at Nashville's annual Fan Fair and how, despite this treatment, Loretta didn't scream. Over and over the writer, Martha Hume, was amazed that Loretta didn't erupt at the merciless demands made upon her:

> Loretta doesn't scream because she's not supposed to. In country music argot she's what's known as a "girl singer," and there are a lot of unwritten rules for girl singers, one of the most important being that no matter how big a star you may be, you may never offend the fans. (57)

The article goes on to describe some typically harrowing days in the life of this "girl singer," who at the time was forty-two, a mother and a grandmother, and a woman responsible for a string of number one hits, many of which she wrote herself.

When k.d. lang told *Maclean's* in early 1985 that "I wanted to do country music . . . but I wanted to be different from the norm" (Hayes), there's little doubt that that difference included freeing herself from the same expectations that hounded Loretta Lynn. And other women in more contemporary country music, such as Rosanne Cash, had the same desire and ran into the same roadblocks as lang when she was questioned about her looks, her commitment, and her choice of material. lang, fighting this brand of sexism and fear of the other, worked the problem into a piece of stage monologue about the expectations placed on a "girl singer":

> When I first got to Nashville . . . I was given a pink handbook on how to be a country-and-western star. Section 1A, the first rule of country-and-western stardom, is, 'The higher the hair, the closer to God.' I tried, but it just wasn't me. (Gillmor 34)

One person who didn't have high hair but had a large reputation and an open welcome for lang to Nashville was Minnie Pearl. As described in *Saturday Night*, Pearl met lang on *Entertainment Tonight* and the two "hit it off." Pearl later explained what she likes about lang:

> "We admire k.d. for her voice and because there is nothing phoney about her. . . . I'm tied to this costume, this persona," she says, surveying her stage-bumpkin dress and the pork-pie Sunday hat in her lap, with its dangling $1.99 price tag. "Not k.d., she's not tied to anything. I think k.d. represents the freedom we all wish we had." (Gillmor 35)

And, of course, her freedom came partly as a result of the trails blazed through the business by women such as Pearl, Rachel Veach, Rose Maddox, Kitty Wells, Patsy Cline, Loretta Lynn, and the list goes on.

By pulling strings with her Opryland representative, Judy Bryte, Minnie Pearl was able to get lang a spot on the Grand Ole Opry in October 1987. At a matinee performance on a bill with Pearl, Roy Acuff, and George Hamilton IV, lang got an encore from a capacity crowd of 4,400. For her encore she did "Crying," which, according to Bryte, "got a standing ovation. It brought the house down. It slaughtered them" (Gillmor 34).

The reason the crowd was so ready to be "slaughtered" by Roy Orbison's old standard was that lang had earlier the same year recorded a duet of the song with Orbison himself, at his invitation, for the soundtrack of the film *Hiding Out* (Rogers 42). That Boston recording session (which had to be finished in Vancouver) led to a video of the song, which in turn, as noted by the *Canadian Composer*, "led to an invitation to appear on a Home Box Office pay-TV special" ("Lang Album Goes Gold"), which has been released as a video called *A Black and White Night* (there's also an album of the same name). Though lang and Orbison do not sing their duet on this latter video, lang does sing back-up with such luminaries as Bonnie Raitt, Jackson Browne, J.D. Souther, and Jennifer Warnes. The band includes Tom Waits, Elvis Costello, and Bruce Springsteen, to name a few. On the CBC's 1992 *Country Gold* program lang pronounced that her duet with Orbison had brought her "baskets of horseshoes" — that since his invitation to sing, her career had really taken off.

On a previous trip to Nashville lang also played the famed Exit/In to a packed house that included the Judds and Lyle Lovett. That exposure got her an invitation to sing as a part of Hank Williams Jr.'s band on the Country Music Awards show. lang was getting big in Nashville, and Gerry Wood's regular "Nashville Scene" column in the 26 September 1987 *Billboard* was titled, "Canada's k.d. lang Gains Acceptance."

Not only did he report, as did all the Canadian papers and trade magazines, on lang's September win of the Canadian Country Music Association's award for Entertainer of the Year and the Vista Rising Star award (in the same month she also won the Alberta Recording Industry Association's Female Vocalist of the Year and Performer of the Year awards), he also raved about her live shows.

Also in this busy year, in time for her twenty-sixth birthday on 2 November, lang's album *Angel with a Lariat* went gold in Canada, "despite," as noted by the *Canadian Composer*, "the fact that it didn't yield a hit single" ("Lang Album Goes Gold"). The album also managed to spend two months on *Billboard*'s Top Country Album chart in mid-1987. Also on her birthday came her second Juno Award, this one for Best Country Female Vocalist of 1987, "breaking," *Alberta Report* proudly announced, "Anne Murray's eight-year lock on the award" (Johnson).

lang headed home in time for Christmas where, according to her mother, Audrey, quoted in *Saturday Night*, she finds "a kind of spiritual renewal," driving the roads around Consort in her four-wheel-drive and riding horses into the hills (Gillmor 34).

Shadowland

One other thing lang managed to squeeze into 1987, which yielded big things in 1988, came as a result of an appearance on *The Tonight Show*, with Johnny Carson. She made her Carson debut in May, and was invited back, thanks to strong audience response. In the meantime, Mary Martin of RCA noticed that despite lang's Nashville exposure, there were still doubts about her. Said Martin to *Saturday Night*, "I think people were suspicious of her. There's still a lot of good ole boys in Nashville and if they think they are being wanked they aren't going to like it. I thought I'd get her and Owen Bradley together and get them less suspicious" (Gillmor 34).

At this point, one might rightfully ask why Mary Martin of RCA took such an interest in an artist under contract to Sire Records, a division of Warner Brothers. Larry Wanagas explains that Martin is a Canadian, from Ontario, who took an interest in lang, another Canadian, when Wanagas was trying to shop for a deal in the U.S. Martin was the only label representative from Nashville who came to hear lang at the Bottom Line, the same time Seymour Stein was there. She wanted to sign lang but couldn't get her RCA bosses to ink a deal. Despite the fact she couldn't get lang, she became an ally of the young singer. Now, back to Nashville.

Owen Bradley, as noted previously, was one of the architects of the Nashville Sound, and a man who'd worked with the likes of Patsy Cline, Kitty Wells, Brenda Lee, and Loretta Lynn. *Esquire* magazine put him in its "Heavy 100 of Country Music" and called him the "Dean of Nashville producers" (Lomax and Oermann 66). As *Saturday Night* remarked, "In an industry that is a genteel pissing contest, Bradley is one of the few people in Nashville about whom no-one has anything ugly to say" (Gillmor 34). Martin noted, quite correctly, that if lang could work with Bradley, the suspicion just might melt away.

Martin told Bradley about lang, but not only had Bradley retired, he'd recently suffered a heart attack, and didn't seem too interested. What followed has become the stuff of country music legend. Here's how *Maclean's* told it:

> Owen Bradley lay awake one night last July [1987], watching a videotape of Johnny Carson on *The Tonight Show*. The legendary 72-year-old record producer . . . was recuperating at his home outside Nashville from a massive heart attack. Doctors insisted on total rest as his only chance for recovery. But Bradley recalls that one of Carson's guests excited him so much that he sat right up in bed. The performer was Canada's k.d. lang. Although Bradley had heard the eccentric country artist's second album, the giddy, up-tempo *Angel with a Lariat*, it was not until he saw her perform an aching rendition of Cline's ballad *Three Cigarettes in an Ashtray* on Carson's show that he realized lang's full potential. Defying his doctors and recovering quickly, Bradley — who had retired in 1980 — went back to work to produce her new record, *Shadowland*. As he writes in the record's liner notes: "After working with k.d. for awhile, I didn't need to take my pills. She was medicine, invigorating therapy." (Jennings and Gregor 58)

Work began on *Shadowland*, lang's third album, in the summer of 1987 for release in the spring of 1988. The album would be a collection of country standards (with one exception), interpreted by lang, produced by Bradley, and backed by the cream of the Nashville session-work crop, players and singers with whom Bradley had worked for years.

As if this wasn't enough to guarantee country respectability, lang teamed up with three giants of the industry, Kitty Wells, Brenda Lee, and Loretta Lynn, for the album's final cut, "Honky Tonk Angels' Medley," comprised of three standards: "In the Evening (When the Sun Goes Down)," "You Nearly Lose Your Mind," and "Blues Stay Away from Me."

Canadian Musician relates that another good reason for lang's working with Bradley was his song selection, and quotes lang on the subject: "He's really into straight ahead lyrics . . . and subject matter everyone can understand. It's almost a totally different school from where I come from. He's opened me up. As a kid I studied Joni Mitchell as a lyricist and hers is a very introspective type of writing. The type of lyrics Owen goes for are very generic and publicly applicable" (Stern, "k.d. lang" 49).

Shadowland has been described by critics and reviewers as "lush" and "romantic," and it is both of those things, with six of its twelve tracks backed by the Nashville String Machine, a large studio ensemble of violins, violas, and cellos that contributes a nostalgic shimmering of fifties pop music feeling to the album. (The ensemble's name, of course, gives plenty of grist to the mill that Nashville is a hit production line.)

The album's range includes the Spanish/western feel of the two stellar songs, "Western Stars" and "Don't Let the Stars Get in Your Eyes"; the honky-tonkin', good time "(Waltz Me) Once Again around the Dance Floor"; the western swing of Bob Wills's "Sugar Moon"; the torchy anguish of veteran jazz/pop writer Frank Loesser's "I Wish I Didn't Love You So"; and the beautiful sultry blues of "Black Coffee." lang has claimed that in her early years she listened to the Allman Brothers, and she repays any debt she owes them with this blues number, much of its tempo and many of its chord changes echoing the Allmans' version of T-Bone Walker's "Stormy Monday Blues."

The last two songs on *Shadowland* are the ones that stirred the greatest interest in the press: "Honky Tonk Angels' Medley" because it was the first time Wells, Lee, and Lynn had been brought together, let alone with newcomer lang, and also because this medley was hoped to be part of a symbolic "letting in" of lang to Nashville; and the second blues cut on the album, "Busy Being Blue." This latter tune is not a country standard but was revived from *a truly western experience*, and it raised eyebrows because it is performed so well.

Both *Rolling Stone* and *Stereo Review* loved the song, the former noting that lang wasn't the least bit intimidated by Owen Bradley's august presence: "[S]he eschews reverent caution and sets off explosions on almost every song, especially

FIGURE 14

A shadowy picture from Shadowland. *By now
lang was recording in the Home of Country Music.*

late-night torch cries like 'Busy Being Blue' " (Guterman, rev. of *Shadowland* 121). Alanna Nash in *Stereo Review* concurred: "She doesn't sing this material so much as she inhabits it, especially the anguished *Too Busy Being Blue* [sic], which she delivers with an explosion of emotion. To say that lang is compelling is only to scratch the surface" ("k.d. lang's Romantic 'Shadowland' " 81).

This was the general run of response to *Shadowland*, though the Americans, once again, had their reservations. This time, at least in the case of the just-mentioned publications, lang was urged to get back together with her band, the reclines, and do some of her own songs, now that she had proved she could go the distance as an interpreter.

Besides veering away from lang's previous course in terms of musical direction, *Shadowland* also took a conservative swing in its visuals. The album's photos are all black-and-white pictures: the artist, in her toned down image, on the front cover; the artist and her producer laughing together, on the back cover; and on the inner sleeve, various photos of the recording sessions underway and of lang sharing a laugh with Bradley, Wells, Lee, and Lynn. This is the stuff of traditional Nashville country albums, along with liner notes of high praise for lang from Bradley and some brief thank-yous from lang to the people she worked with, and to Patsy Cline.

Despite the almost unbelievable opportunity of working with Bradley, with Wells, Lee, and Lynn, and with Bradley's network of famous musicians; despite the fact that lang had toned down her image and had concentrated on her singing, which *Maclean's* noticed when it entered her on its Honor Roll in December 1988, speaking of her "rich, expressive and superbly controlled alto voice" ("New Fame" 15); despite all the raves for her live performances and the critical kudos she received for *Shadowland*; despite all this, in the words of *This Magazine* ". . . K.D. remain[ed] an outsider in the town that proudly hails itself as Music City, U.S.A." (Hawthorn 15).

Saturday Night also noted this phenomenom: "One reviewer suggested that if Dolly Parton had recorded *Shadowland* there would be a ticker-tape parade down the streets of Nashville. There wasn't a parade for lang; the town kept its distance"

(Gillmor 34). Only two singles were released from the album and they got a minimum of airplay. "It's a very big disappointment that it didn't get played more," said Owen Bradley. "I can't explain it" (Gillmor 34). He then went on to provide a possible explanation. "I was in Atlanta, and some of the people there, they love the songs, but they don't like the image. That comes up quite a bit. . . . I think she's winning slowly but surely. She's just outsinging them, and, you know, that's the hard way to do it. But she'll do it. She's just outsinging them and that's the hardest way of all to go" (Gillmor 34–35).

lang was doing it the way she'd said she'd do it: on her own terms. "I think I've been successful," she told *Saturday Night*. "I play to sold-out audiences and I play my music in uncompromising terms. I think that's as successful as one can ask for. In terms of formulated success, having hit singles and selling lots of records, that's not where I'm successful" (Gillmor 35).

Chatelaine's Woman of the Year

One tangible sign of this success, for Canadians, anyway, was that between the recording and the release of *Shadowland*, in January 1988, lang was named *Chatelaine* magazine's Woman of the Year. Said lang, in *This Magazine*, of the choice: "It was quite a big step for them to put someone like me on the cover, because I'm not a stereotypical woman. . . . I think it's really cool. . . . I think it's great because they allowed me to be myself. The only unfortunate thing is that they airbrushed lipstick, but I guess that was their last laugh" (Hawthorn 15).

This Magazine responded by commenting that "[b]are lips on female singers seems to be too much of a challenge for some" (Hawthorn 15). And that's likely just the tip of the iceberg. Bare lips are part of lang's carefully studied androgynous image, upon which everyone from *Maclean's* to *Stereo Review* has commented, and around which much of the grumbling and suspicion in the country music industry still swirls. Her "unconventional sexual presentation," as Ann Magnuson described it in *Elle*, and her standing up "for her differentness" (80), would take on a new cast with lang's 1992 announcement that she was a lesbian. But in 1988, in *Chatelaine's* Woman of the Year article, lang explained her image in this way: "I'm a very androgynous-looking woman, and my goals are not to be a wife or necessarily a mother. Androgyny is important in my life because I can deal with people on a human, not a sexual, level; it's important on stage, because both men and women are attracted to me. . . . It's important not to eliminate possibilities for people" (Scott 132).

Eliminating possibilities is exactly what the country radio people seem to have in mind, however, to keep everything controlled and safe. lang has won her converts, though. Kitty Wells was quoted in *Maclean's* as saying of lang, "You've got to have something that's all your own if you want to stand out. . . . And she has an originality that makes her unique" (Jennings and Gregor 59). lang, in the words of Bradley, just has to keep "outsinging them."

She did that, with appearances across the U.S. and Europe through the summer of 1988 and an appearance with the Amnesty International Tour when it came to Toronto in September 1988, playing with the likes of Sting, Bruce Springsteen, Peter Gabriel, and Tracy Chapman. Perhaps her most famous 1988 appearance, however, goes back to February when she helped close the Winter Olympics at Calgary. Tom Hawthorn of *This Magazine* is hilarious on the subject:

> An eternity in Hell can't be much worse than two hours in front of the tube watching the closing ceremonies of Calgary's Winter Olympics. It was a schlockathon of corny costumes, marshmallow music and saccharine song that featured skaters in turn-of-the-century clothes, skaters in trailing red capes and skaters dressed like Mounties in scarlet tunics and forest ranger hats and fake legless horses that fit around their waist. It was as if a lawn full of ornaments had suddenly come to life.
>
> Not until the skating Mounties appeared did the ceremony have anything at all to do with the country in which it was being held. For the 60,000 at the stadium and the two billion supposedly watching on television, this exercise in silliness may as well have been held on a backlot in the Hollywood hills.

FIGURE 15

lang at Amnesty International concert [Toronto, 1988].

Then K.D. came a-burstin' onstage to sing "Turn Me Round." While she do-si-doed and let out fierce whoops, the athletes poured down from the stands for an impromptu square dance. She did a high-falutin' high-step that brought a roar from the crowd and even more manic dancing from the jocks. And then, as her song came to an end, a breathless K.D. leaned into two billion television sets to say, simply, "Peace." She even flashed the old two-fingered peace sign from the sixties. It was corny as hell, but she meant it. (16–17)

Adding to an already high-profile year, lang won triple honours at the Canadian Country Music Awards in September, for Entertainer, Female Vocalist, and Album of the Year. She also picked up a CASBY (Canadian Artists Selected By You — an alternative to the Junos) Award in October for Female Vocalist of the Year, and a Gemini (Canadian television) in November for Best Performance in a TV Variety (for the Country Music Awards). As well, *Rolling Stone* named her its Best New Female Vocalist in its Magazine Critics' Poll.

Absolute Torch and Twang

In rainy December Vancouver, lang capped off 1988 with another trip to the recording studio, and album number four.

For *Absolute Torch and Twang* lang got back together with the reclines, who had been put on hold, so to speak, while lang did *Shadowland*. She'd wanted her band for the Nashville album, but Bradley, according to *Canadian Musician*, didn't want to have to work out a communication system with a new group of musicians. Says lang: "I think the Reclines were put off at first but I think they realize now it was an opportunity I had to fulfill" (Stern, "k.d. lang" 49). The reclines, by now, included only one original member, guitarist Gordie Matthews. Drummer Michel Pouliot (it was Miche on *Angel*) and Mink were holdovers from *Angel with a Lariat*.

This time lang would be recording where she lived, and she would be sitting in the producer's chair, beside bandmate Ben Mink and a new producer, Greg Penny. Penny's credentials were slender, but they were just right for lang. He came up from Los Angeles with one dance single, "Martini Beach," to his credit, and a "solid background in traditional country music, bathed in youthful enthusiasm," in the words of *Alberta Report* (Remple 51).

The songs on *Absolute Torch and Twang* are a fairly eclectic mix of styles, tempos, and subject matter, eight of them penned by lang and Mink, one by lang, and three from the great store of country standards to which lang has ready access.

The album, which was completed and released in the spring of 1989, opens with the soft but insistent beat of "Luck in My Eyes," the gentle imagery of a "mountain rain" building to a "howling wind" and then lang's full-throated declaration: "all my troubles, all my troubles, gone / with luck in my eyes." From this personal statement, lang turns to the Willie Nelson/ Faron Young composition "Three Days," a honky-tonkin' tune chock-full of high vocal energy and anguish. Then there's "Trail of Broken Hearts," a haunting, slowly loping song with the western whine of the steel guitar recalling some of the eeriness of the old instrumental "(Ghost) Riders in the Sky," as played, for instance, by the Ventures on *Another Smash*.

"Big Boned Gal" is a happy, head-high, fiddle-charged dance tune about an independent woman in a small Alberta town who could hold the locals in a trance when she got up to dance, and it sounds fairly autobiographical. "Didn't I," with its echoing refrain, is a tense, guitar-powered song about modern unrequited love, while "Wallflower Waltz" goes back to an old-time, country waltz for its structure and features lang singing in a pained voice about leaning against the wall waiting to be asked to dance. lang told *Chatelaine* that "Wallflower Waltz" was "about accepting yourself and not striving to be an image invented by other people" (Scott 132).

"Full Moon Full of Love," by Jeannie Smith and Leroy Preston, has a happy, western swing feel to it, and "Pullin' Back the Reins" goes straight into the slow and mournful blues, reaching for, and completely filling, every note.

lang heads for the dance floor, big time, with Wynn Stewart's "Big Big Love," then makes a classic, artist-answering-her-fans-and-family statement, in "It's Me." Here lang sings:

> what you see on t.v.
> all them sparkles
> it ain't me
>
> .   .   .   .
>
> i'm not asking for the world
> i just want to be an ordinary girl
> might not be all you want
> but it's all you get, it's me

Many an artist has made this declaration of woe, trying to separate the media image from the person who walked into it all in the first place. Kathy Naylor, lang's old basketball coach, says, good-naturedly, she doesn't believe the words of this song at all. It's not hard to imagine that lang, when one considers how far she's taken herself, hardly pines, really and truly, just to be "an ordinary girl." But, it's a measure of lang's immersion in the music business that by her fourth album she is yearning for a little release, however occasional.

"Walkin' in and out of Your Arms" is a song about independence in a love relationship, replete with western imagery. In fact, a large part of the album is devoted to both love relationships and western imagery. The final song, "Nowhere to Stand," was written by lang alone, and its moody and troubled strings help deliver a message about child abuse. lang's words are blunt, to the point, and go to her own backyard for their example:

> a family tradition
> the strength of this land
> where what's right and wrong
> is the back of a hand
> turns girls into women
> a boy to a man
> but the rights of the children
> have nowhere to stand

This is not the stuff that country radio programmers, or e[...]
rock programmers, would rush to play. Alanna Nash, in [...]
highly favourable review of *Absolute Torch and Twang* in
Stereo Review, having remarked on the exceptional qualities
of "Nowhere to Stand" with its "emotional plea for child-abuse
laws," concluded of the album as a whole: "In a time when only
a handful of artists challenge country music to rise from its
stagnant, if comfortable, mire of conservatism, k.d. lang is in
there with a cattle prod." Holly Gleason in *Rolling Stone* said
much the same thing: "This album isn't gonna win her any
points with the Nashville Network or country-radio programmers, but it shows what country music, when intelligently
done, can be: high-plains music for the thinking man and
woman" (166).

In *Canadian Living* magazine, lang explained how she felt
about *Absolute Torch and Twang*: "This . . . is probably the first
time I have ever truly revealed that many aspects of me: the
writing, the production, being absolutely myself on the
cover. . . . I feel a little more at ease gaining a certain level of
acceptance. It relaxes me" (Stanley and Nicholson 38).

The cover is a simple colour shot of lang, dressed in blue jeans
and western-style leather coat over a denim jacket, holding a
cowboy hat and a pair of gloves, and standing in an Alberta
wheat field. On the back of the CD booklet is a black and white
shot of lang in full cowboy regalia — including hat, scarf,
embroidered shirt, leather chaps, and boots — tending a fire,
set against a studio backdrop of trees and a sunset.

lang also commented to *Canadian Living* about acknowledg-
ing her Alberta roots: "The songs are about Alberta, and the
video and the album cover are shot in Alberta because that's
what I like. I like the Prairies. I like grain elevators. It's not to
promote Alberta — that's definitely the wrong word. . . . But
this is where I'm from and this is where most of the imagery in
my music and performance comes from. And most of my
humor is Canadian" (Stanley and Nicholson 38).

Another thing lang's new album did was put a title before the
public for her brand of music: torch and twang. After all, she'd
expressed her dissatisfaction with "cowpunk," "punkabilly,"
and with being included under the "New Traditionalists" head-

k Times said of her new label, "The torch side
nality blends the smooth perfection of Anne
ritty directness of Patsy Cline. Her twangy
...lls Elvis Presley" (Holden).

...ule, back on the awards circuit, lang won her first
Grammy Award (National Academy of Recording Arts and
Sciences) in March 1989, for Best Country Vocal Collaboration.
The prize was for "Crying," her duet with the, by now, late Roy
Orbison. In the same month she won Juno awards for Female
Vocalist of the Year and Country Female Vocalist of the Year
and won the *Rolling Stone* Critics' Pick for Best Female Singer,
in a tie with Tracy Chapman.

k.d. lang's Buffalo Cafe

In June 1989 lang headed for Sylvan Lake, Alberta, a resort
community about 150 kilometers northwest of Edmonton, to
begin filming a CBC television special, *k.d. lang's Buffalo Cafe*.
Filming also took place at a tavern in Red Deer (the Quality
Inn), but not in the actual Buffalo Tavern, a country music bar
lang knew from her college days. Unfortunately, the real
McCoy didn't have an adequate power supply, so down the
street went the CBC cameras.

The special was released in November and featured, along
with lang, comedian Susan Norfleet, who plays a receptionist
in the Buffalo Hotel who mistakes lang for a man when lang
checks in; Dwight Yoakam, who's had his own share of trouble
with Nashville; and Stompin' Tom Connors. Connors performed his new tune "Lady, k.d. lang," a song he wrote in her
honour. Connors told *Canadian Living*, "I think a lot of what
she stands for and what she's doing. . . . Canada needs this kind
of shot in the arm" (Stanley and Nicholson 41). lang feels
Connors is an "important Canadian folk hero" who was driven
out of the music business by a lack of support for his kind of
music. "I think that 15 years ago," explains lang, "Canadians
suffered from a very big case of insecurity and lack of self-
confidence dealing with culture on an international level, but

things are different now" (Stanley and Nicholson 41).

Part of that difference, and that confidence, comes from lang, but she knows it took a Stompin' Tom to help clear the way for her. *k.d. lang's Buffalo Cafe*, and particularly Connors's segment, was a real hootenanny, and it later won two Emmy awards, for Best Variety Program and Best Variety Performance.

Prior to the special's release, lang picked up three Canadian Country Music awards for Best Female Vocalist, Best Album, and Entertainer of the Year, in September 1989. Six months later, in March 1990, she won a Grammy Award for Best Female Country Vocalist. In the same month, *Rolling Stone's* Critics' Pick named her Country Artist of the Year. It looked as if things would just keep getting better. Well, they didn't.

Despite her Grammy win, which usually means big things in the U.S., a headline in the 10 March 1990 *Billboard* read, "Country PDs [program directors] Resist Grammy Winners" (Ross 14). The winners were lang and Lyle Lovett, another artist with whom country radio has difficulty. Despite, as well, the fact that lang's *Absolute Torch and Twang* was selling strongly, as reported in *Billboard*, and that she was a favourite of the "consumer press and country video outlets" (Ross 14), she wasn't making any headway on country radio.

Nick Hunter, Warner Brothers senior vice-president of national country sales/promotion, acknowledges that "the image lang projects scares the living hell out of country radio. She doesn't have hair piled on top of her head. She doesn't look like the rest of them and that intimidates people" (Ross 85). lang told an interviewer in *Glamour* magazine, around the same time, "Men aren't used to a woman responding aggressively the way I do. We all know that an aggressive woman is considered a bitch but aggression in a man is a good business trait" (Krupp). Country radio, and the country music business in general, had been pushing women around for years. Now here was one that not only wasn't going to take it, her very appearance was scaring them to boot. One look, for instance, at the video of "Ridin' the Rails," the jazzy-pop tune she, along with vocal group Take 6, contributed in 1990 to the *Dick Tracy* soundtrack, and you can see how far she's distanced herself from the Judds and the Mandrell sisters. In this video lang is dressed like a young man, forties style, with her hair slicked back, thus exuding what she later called a "cryptic sexuality" (Kohanov 74).

Beef Stinks

On top of this resistance to her image, lang unleashed a proverbial storm of protest with an advertisement she made in Los Angeles.

In her January 1988 Woman of the Year article in *Chatelaine* lang said, "But even with my strong beliefs that are not old-fashioned — about vegetarianism, for instance — I try to be open to other people. When I go out to Consort with my cowboy friends from childhood and round up cattle, I lecture them a little on vegetarianism, but at the same time, I can't lecture. I believe the strongest example in everything is a silent example" (Scott 132).

lang must have grown impatient with that approach for in June 1990 she filmed a commercial for People for the Ethical Treatment of Animals (PETA). In her ad, part of a campaign which included clips from Paul McCartney and the B-52s, lang stands beside a cow named Lulu and implores people to give up meat. Part of the text of the commercial runs, "We all love animals, but why do we call some pets and some dinner? If you knew how meat was made, you'd lose your lunch. I know. I'm from cattle country and that's why I became a vegetarian" (Stevenson 19).

Though the ad would not be broadcast in Canada and was not to be broadcast in the U.S. till late summer of 1990 (and, according to her manager, Larry Wanagas, never did run in the U.S.), word of it got out, thanks to *Entertainment Tonight*, and the howls of protest started in the early summer. Radio stations in Alberta and Nebraska, beef areas both, pulled lang from their playlists — though, just as significantly, many didn't. Back home in Consort, lang's mother was subjected to abusive phone calls and the Home of k.d. lang sign on the edge of town was defaced. *Alberta Report* (published outside the province as *Western Report*), which had always behaved like a personal cheering section for lang, pulled an about-face and titled its first story on the uproar "K.D. the Cow-Hugger" (Stevenson 19). The story featured the comment from an unidentified employee at lang's management company, Bumstead Productions, in Vancouver, that lang and her people hadn't expected all the negative publicity. Even die-hard fans found this hard to believe.

Two weeks later, *Alberta Report*'s 23 July 1990 issue featured lang on its cover with Lulu the cow and the headline "K.D.'s Cow Pie." The accompanying four-page story, plus an impassioned letter from the publisher, combined to give an impression of Albertans aghast at the betrayal of one of their key industries by a homegrown daughter. If lang's naïveté at the uproar she'd created was hard to believe, *Alberta Report*'s new reading on the woman and music it had once championed was just as unbelieveable: "[D]espite her tremendous singing voice, few liked her songs to begin with" (Taylor 32).

Three weeks later, the letters column in *Alberta Report* was divided on the harm, if any, lang had done to the local beef industry. Meanwhile, south of the border, *Musician* magazine editor Bill Flanagan, in an article in *Billboard*, denounced the policy of stations that had banned lang's records for her anti-beef-eating stance as censorship and, worse, as un-American. Later, in August, a commentary in *Billboard* was headlined "[Recording] Industry Should Defend K.D. Lang's Rights" (Abelson).

By September 1991, *Alberta Report* seemed to be back on lang's side, claiming her as "Alberta's cowpunker" (Christie), giving her film debut a boost, and mentioning that she was at work on a new album. In late December the magazine ran an article on new research that showed cows are not causing the global warming of which they were once accused. The article mentioned the PETA organization for whom lang filmed her ad, but no mention was made of lang, though a gratuitous swipe could easily have been made. The bad methane smell in the air seemed to have cleared, though an article in the April 1992 *Musician* claimed lang still hadn't fully recovered: "I went from being Canada's little queen to all of a sudden having the whole country against me. It's a little scary to feel that wave shift" (Rogers 40–41).

Later still, in June 1992, lang cancelled a concert scheduled for Owen Sound, Ontario, because of vehement protests from local beef producers. Whereas the general manager of the Canadian Cattlemen's Association, Dennis Laycraft, commented from Calgary that lang's advertisement had had no effect on the beef industry and that her message was not to be taken very seriously (Ionides), it seems that others did not share his opinion.

lang's Film Debut

The film debut heralded in September 1991 by *Alberta Report* was of *Salmonberries*, a film written and directed by German-born Percy Adlon, director of *Sugarbaby* and *Bagdad Cafe*. lang had met Adlon after she'd seen *Bagdad Cafe* and requested that he make the video of her contribution to *Red Hot + Blue*. This latter was a collection of Cole Porter songs covered by a variety of modern artists, including U2, David Byrne, and Fine Young Cannibals, as both a tribute to Porter and a benefit to AIDS research and awareness.

Though lang had yet to make a public declaration of her lesbianism, and though one hardly needs to be either a lesbian or a homosexual to make a contribution to combatting AIDS and the prejudices that fan out from it, lang once again stood up publicly for her beliefs. She would later comment to Brendan Lemon in *The Advocate* when he asked her about the political ramifications of AIDS and the *Red Hot + Blue* project: "[T]he fact that anyone could say that AIDS is God's way of paying back homosexuals is really disturbing. If that's true, then lesbians are angels" (40).

lang recorded her cover of Porter's "So in Love" in Vancouver in the late summer of 1990 with Mink, Penny, and herself behind the production boards. John Carlin, in his notes to *Red Hot + Blue*, says of Porter, "His music presents love as a personal, almost subversive, force that enables us to transcend life's hardships." This definition would appeal to lang, who has many times been called a subversive in the music industry and who sings many a love song. Some of Porter's lyrics, however, which lang takes from a breathy introduction to a powerful ending, all set to a slow rhumba beat, seem much too masochistic for the k.d. lang who's been doing things her own way for so long. "So taunt me and hurt me, / deceive me, desert me, / I'm yours 'til I die," doesn't sound true to form, though the lines "how long till i panic / how long do i wait," from lang's "Didn't I," begin to enter similar territory. Nonetheless, lang's performance, in many people's opinion, was one of the strongest on the album, up there with Sinead O'Connor's and the Neville Brothers's.

Working with lang on the *Red Hot + Blue* video inspired Adlon to create a film around a character written specifically for lang. Adlon, as quoted in *Country* magazine, says he took one look at lang and felt as if he'd been "struck by lightning" (Griffin 11). He told Vickie Gabereau on her CBC radio show, in February 1992, that it was lang's eyes that did it to him.

Salmonberries is about Kotz (lang), a 20-year-old, boyish-looking, half-white, half-Inuit foundling who lives in Kotzebue, Alaska, and is searching for her roots and identity. According to *Alberta Report*, she is an "explosive, alienated character who . . . is drawn to a middle-aged German lady librarian, played by costar Rosel Zech" (Christie 41). Montreal *Gazette* film critic John Griffin, as paraphrased in *Alberta Report*, says, "The plot . . . revolves around a frustrated lesbian relationship that is not consummated because the older woman will not have it" (Christie 41). *Salmonberries* associate producer Beverly Graf claims that the story is "not a torrid lesbian romance. . . . It is a relationship between two women and there is a sexual cast to it" ("Film Starring Lang").

Filming took place at Kotzebue, on the Bering Sea, for six weeks in late 1990 and for a further three weeks in Berlin the same year. The film was conceived, according to Adlon, as the Berlin wall came down and the Germanies were reunified. "Those events give a political subtext . . . to a movie about breaking down barriers at a personal level" (Christie 41).

Salmonberries, which takes its title from the jars of Alaskan berries the German librarian keeps around her room, won the Best Film award at the Montreal World Film Festival in September 1991. It has gone on to other film festivals and is making its way, with considerable success, around Europe, but lang's manager, Larry Wanagas, says it's unlikely North Americans will get to see it because there has been a lot of trouble securing a deal with a distributor on this continent.

Out of the *Salmonberries* project, however, came a new single and video of a song lang does near the end of the movie, though she does not appear in the film as a singer. The song is called "Barefoot" and was cowritten by lang and Bob Telson, who wrote "Calling You," one of the high points of *Bagdad Cafe*. The single was released in Germany and the video made it onto the CBC's *Dan Gallagher's Video Hits* on 3 January 1992. In "Barefoot," a song with a sparse arrangement of acoustic guitar and some strings, lang sings, "I'd walk through the snow barefoot / If you'd open your door," then, near the end, breaks into a howl. The video cuts to husky dogs charging through the snow to drive home the parallel between the aching lover and the panting dogs. This is torch-song yearning taken to a new level.

Regarding more acting, Larry Wanagas was quoted in *Alberta Report* as saying lang would welcome it as long as it didn't interfere with her music (Christie 41). And it was her music that won her the Canadian Academy of Recording Arts and Sciences (CARAS) trophy for Female Artist of the Decade, on 20 November 1991. (The previous, and first, winner of the award was Anne Murray.)

For a good part of the decade k.d. lang dominated the Canadian entertainment press, and other news areas, and eventually the country's awards ceremonies — in her categories, of course. She also took categories in general, be they music, gender, fashion, or behaviour, and gave then a vigorous stretching, much to the betterment of the music, of categories, and of the Canadian sense of humour. lang was an obvious choice for Artist of the Decade.

FIGURE 16

lang on Saturday Night Live, *1992*

"Wait till you see . . . the '90s"

"[I]f women are going to be crazy, who's gonna make lunch?" (Hammond 37)

When k.d. lang received her Artist of the Decade award, the final words of her acceptance speech were, according to Richard Flohil in the *Canadian Composer*, "I've just started to walk. Wait till you see what I do in the '90s!" ("k.d.").

With *Salmonberries*, and words about her interest in more acting, lang revealed some of what she'd do in the next decade. With her new album, *Ingénue*, released in March 1992, she lived up to a pronouncement she made about herself a month earlier on CBC's *Country Gold*: "[P]eople always knew I was . . . going to make a right turn at any second."

One has to assume from her statement that a right turn means a complete turning away from country music to the realm where easy-listening jazz and adult-oriented pop music cross paths — much the kind of realm she was in when she contributed "So in Love" to the *Red Hot + Blue* album. Indeed, Ben Mink claims in a *Musician* article that "the *Red Hot + Blue* track was a real key, a cornerstone to this [the *Ingénue*] album" (Rogers 38).

lang told the CBC's Peter Gzowski in a 20 March 1992 *Morningside* interview that, while the silly and fun part of her is still there, *Ingénue* shows another side. Now that she's thirty, she told Gzowski, she wants to move on into different territory. As her June 1992 interview with Brendan Lemon in *The Advocate* made clear, she had long been inhabiting a territory different from the one a significant portion of the public perceived. Lemon prefaced his interview with this description of how lang responded to questions about her sexuality: "Consistently, lang has been reticent about certain subjects, her sexuality in particular. She just assumed that we all got it, and when she was asked questions about it, her responses ranged from deflective firmness . . . to deflective irony . . ." (36).

In one sense, *Ingénue* carries on the torch-song tradition of lang's earlier output, but here yearning and craving are carried to greater extremes — the album is about the pain of love, because, as she told Gzowski, love is painful. In response to another interviewer's comment that *Ingénue* was "definitely more torch than twang," lang responded, "It's love. Yeah, love. Pure, unrequited, unconsummated love" (Magnuson 80), and Jeff Bateman, in *Network*, paraphrased lang on the subject of her inspiration for the album: "It's based on a real relationship, . . . one that has dragged her heart around and painfully resolved itself over the last two years" (25). lang's interview with *The Advocate* put an end to much speculation by indicating that the object of lang's unrequited love was a married woman (Lemon 36).

The yearning lang pours into *Ingénue* is relentless, no longer broken up by sidetrips into dance tunes and rock-and-country wailers. In fact, on only three cuts does she employ a full drum kit, relying mostly on various percussion devices and a beat box. And only on the final cut, "Constant Craving," does she break out of the tones of blue and languorous resignation that dominate the album to that point and really bust loose with some rhythmically sunny optimism — despite the song's title.

Which isn't to say that the preceding songs are dreary. lang and fellow-producers Ben Mink and Greg Penny manage to dress lyrics about pain — wounds, shame, "kisses of sin," a "hollow soul," doubts, endurance, and tears — in such intoxicating rhythms and melodies that listeners are quickly seduced by the sound. A prime example is the opener, "Save Me," in which the lyrics call out for deliverance while the music's languid mood completely negates the verbal message. Of note at this point is that lang appears to have turned away from the "generic and publicly applicable" (Stern, "k.d. lang" 49) lyrics she embraced in the *Shadowland* sessions and returned to the introspection of a much earlier songwriting hero, Joni Mitchell. And Mitchell, another prairie Canadian, must be a hero, for lang told Brendan Lemon that "Joni Mitchell's the only person with whom I've ever been star-struck" (42).

lang and company (not the reclines — "The Reclines had developed a certain sound," said lang, "it was a country sound and I just wanted to change" [Rogers 38]) bring in instruments such as vibraphone, marimba, cello, and clarinet, and turn the fiddle and the accordion from their former country leanings to

FIGURE 17

lang on Saturday Night Live *doing a song from* Ingénue.
That's Ben Mink behind her with the electric violin.

a more Eurasian direction. There's the oriental violin sound of "The Mind of Love" and "So It Shall Be," the Latin beat of "Still Thrives This Love," and the Parisian feel of "Miss Chatelaine."

The album cover is swathed in grainy images of an abject-looking lang, easily the picture of unrequited or unsettled love, while the music inside begs for the romance of old ballrooms and thirties musicals, of Amelia Earhart and China Clipper flying boats, of Parisian cafes and Middle-Eastern oases, or at least Hollywood's ideas of these things. Which brings the listener back around to the album's title, *Ingénue*, generally understood as a stage role in which the actor plays the part of a guileless or innocent young woman, making wrong turns everywhere in the maze of love.

One part of the maze of love that lang is likely happy to have escaped is that in which the press made endless speculations about her sexuality. It's a sad fact of a generally homophobic society that lang has had to fight hard against being categorized by the music industry in order to keep her sexuality "cryptic" (Kohanov 74) so as not to "eliminate possibilities for people" (Scott 132). lang explained to Brendan Lemon that the stage gave her "emancipation to do things" (42), that there, to para-phrase lang, her art could transcend sex, but still retain sexual elements (Lemon 42). Lemon responded to this idea by asking, "But how can your art ever transcend your sexuality?" to which lang replied, "Only in the fact that I would hope I can attract both men and women. And that when a person is attracted to me, they're not thinking about my genitals" (42).

Following lang's announcement in print of her lesbianism and the flurry of headlines and television clips that accompanied it, there came more relaxed articles that carried such headlines as, "Lang Happy with Reaction to Recent Admission." The articles then went on to devote the majority of their space to lang's new musical direction and the tour she was undertaking to promote *Ingénue*. "Singing is everything to me," said lang, "and all the rest of the stuff, all the controversy, all the adversity, all the work, everything — it means nothing compared to singing" (Stevenson, "Lang Says Music").

So lang, to a great degree, has become what she told Larry Wanagas she wanted to be when they first met: a jazz singer.

She told *Maclean's* in December 1988 about other things she'd like to have in her future: "I've got a lot of dreams, and they don't all revolve around music. I'd like to be a farmer. I'd like to be an actress, a painter, a motorcycle mechanic. I dream every night that I play for the [Edmonton] Oilers" ("New Fame" 15). Her musical collaborator Ben Mink told *Pulse!* magazine in 1992, "There's no limit to what she can do. . . . I think she's one of the finest vocalists the world has ever seen. The sound of that voice is a miracle, and I think her maturity and interpretation will keep on growing" (Kohanov 77).

All of which goes to say that the future for lang will likely be as varied as her past. Take a look at her 1991 video collection, *k.d. lang: Harvest of Seven Years (Cropped and Chronicled)*, and you see and hear the immense variety, the amazing voice, and the craziness (which Marie-Lynn Hammond, one-time member of Stringband and a CBC radio host, says is "simply imagination taken off its leash" [37]).

lang's imagination has refused to be leashed — or bridled, to pursue the implications of the metaphor in "Pullin' Back the Reins." She won legions of fans for a genre of music that many thought was dull and corny by not taking herself too seriously and by having fun. As of 1992, emerging country musicians such as Michelle Wright ("Country Gold") and Cassandra Vasik ("Dan Gallagher's Video Hits") credit her with clearing the way for them in a business which newspaper and magazine articles everywhere claim is the genre of the future, the genre lang has left behind. While working with country music she refused to be marketed as a "girl singer," sticking instead to her androgynous appearance and rankling on narrow minds everywhere.

She went against industry wisdom and sang an unmarketable song for an old friend on her first album (and she comes back to him, singing "Drifter and me, we've got some plans," in the slow blues jam that concludes *k.d. lang's Buffalo Cafe*). On *Absolute Torch and Twang* she sang a song about child abuse and the cycle of violence on her home turf. She took a public stand on her beliefs about the ethical treatment of animals and about AIDS. Perhaps, as *Saturday Night* suggested when it spoke of Nashville not entirely embracing k.d. lang, she "needs a conservative windmill to tilt at" (Gillmor 35). Indeed, she told

Terry David Mulligan on a 1992 MuchMusic special, "I'd make more ripples if I wasn't concerned about my family."

And where has all this quixotic behaviour gotten her? When I told people I was writing this biography, nearly every one of them told me that they loved k.d. lang, and then went on to tell me why. Saskatoon playwright and poet Don Kerr told me *Shadowland* never left his family's turntable for about a year, and that it's still close by. Another Saskatonian, novelist and screenwriter Sharon Riis, told me she has nothing but admiration for lang, for her uncompromising stand, for her unwillingness to cave in to the appeal of irony when she does an old country song. "She may look wild, she may have crazy props, but she sings it straight and true." Joyce Roberts, president of the Saskatoon SPCA, told me enthusiastically that she loves lang's music and greatly admires her for taking the stand she did on the ethical treatment of animals. "This woman is willing to endure a plunge in sales to stand up for her beliefs. I don't see that willingness to take a cut in pay happening with most other people, even well-off ones, who supposedly love animals." And Larry Kjearsgaard, principal of Consort School, told me on the phone in June 1992 that despite all that's been said about Kathy Lang, "We're all just damn proud of her here."

A 1984 article in *Alberta Report* quoted a Toronto industry insider who warned that lang's talent would soon outrun the abilities of a manager like Larry Wanagas. The insider suggested a remedy and talked about the "mega-dollars" to be made. lang countered that she did not want to make "mega-dollars" and defined her notion of success: ". . . I want the freedom to indulge myself in the arts. All this could look like a hard act to follow, but you can never really plan anything. You can't plan how much a rose is going to grow, and people aren't any different" (Philip, Whyte, and Cohen 45). Wise words from a young woman who defied so-called good business sense and followed her own path, her own schedule, indulging herself in the arts, and still doing so, by the way, with her original manager.

lang's own path has also taken her to her new permanent residence, a farm outside Vancouver (though she often temporarily resides in Los Angeles) with a variety of animals and a

Harley Davidson motorcycle. When asked by Johnny Carson on the 3 April 1992 edition of *The Tonight Show* if it was a "working farm," lang replied, "It works for me."

Margaret Atwood is quoted in the *Canadian Composer* as saying, "You can't defy convention, you can't counter tradition. Unless, of course, you are very good. k.d. lang is *very* good" (Flohil, "k.d."). Personally, I like Winnipeg poet Di Brandt's lines at the end of her essay in *Language in Her Eye*:

> driving home in the car after a k.d. lang concert at Bird's Hill Park in July. my blood beating with her music, her flashing silver sequined jacket, her powerful, her incredible voice. . . .
>
> . . . so what is it, i ask [my daughters] in the car, after, driving home, what is it that k.d. lang has, that those other singers didn't have? (Lisa, who loves Marilyn Monroe & wears her blonde hair in a wave over her forehead, & Ali, who's covered the ballerina wallpaper in her room with Madonna photos.) *fashion & passion*, says Ali, promptly, who is ten, & knows. (57–58)

Ableson, Jeffrey. "Industry Should Defend K.D. Lang's Rights." *Billboard* 18 Aug. 1990: 11.

"Alta. Resort Town Enjoys Filming of Lang TV Special." *StarPhoenix* [Saskatoon] 20 June 1989: E6.

"AR This Week." *Alberta Report* 3 Dec. 1984: 3.

Atherly, Ruth. "K.D. Lang." *Maclean's* 6 July 1987: 36.

Augustson, Nola. Telephone interview. 17 Dec. 1991.

A Black and White Night: Roy Orbison and Friends. Videocassette. Dir. Tony Mitchell. Prod. Stephanie Bennett. Exec. prod. Barbara Orbison. HBO Video, 1988. 15 songs.

Bateman, Jeff. "Ben Mink: 'We Just Went with the Rain.'" *Canadian Composer* 1992: 5

——. "Between Dusk and Dawn: k.d. lang's New Horizon." *Network* [Toronto] Apr.–May 1992: 24–25, 26.

Brandt, Di. "letting the silence speak." *Language in Her Eye: Writing and Gender.* Ed. Libby Scheier, Sarah Sheard, and Eleanor Wachtel. Toronto: Coach House, 1990. 54–58.

Byfield, Link. "Behind 'Animal Rights' Lies the Morality of the Jungle." *Alberta Report* 23 July 1990: 4.

Caldwell, Linda, and Richard Geoffries. "Stompin' Her Way to Glory." *Alberta Report* 2 Mar. 1987: 50.

"Canadian Cowpunk." *Rolling Stone* 20 June 1985: 18.

Carlin, John. Liner notes. *Red Hot + Blue.* Various artists. Chrysalis, F2 21799, 1990.

Christie, Romie. "K.D. Lang as Eskimo." *Alberta Report* 16 Sept. 1991: 41.

Country Gold. Narr. Peter Gzowski. Writ. Martha Kehoe. Prod. and Dir. Joan Tosoni. CBC Variety Special. CBKST, Saskatoon. 1 and 2 Feb. 1992.

Delaney, Larry. Rev. of *a truly western experience,* by k.d. lang and the reclines. *Country Music News* Feb. 1985: 14.

Dellar, Fred, Roy Thompson, and Douglas B. Green. *The Illustrated Encyclopedia of Country Music.* New York: Harmony, 1977.

Dolphin, Ric, ed. "Albertans." *Alberta Report* 5 Dec. 1983: 31.

Dougherty, Steve, and Kristina Johnson. "Quirky K.D. Lang Steps Out as Country Music's Latest Hit Kicker." *People* 4 July 1988: 94–96.

Elash, Anita. "NY [Loves] KD." *Alberta Report* 13 May 1985: 43.

Eremo, Judie, ed. *Country Musicians*. Cupertino, CA: GPI, 1987.

"Farmers' Beef Cans k.d.'s Concert." *Toronto Star* 14 June 1992: A18.

"Film Starring Lang to Be in Competition at Montreal Festival." *StarPhoenix* [Saskatoon] 11 June 1991: D4.

Flanagan, Bill. "Radio Moo-ves to Ban Anti-Beef lang Are Un-American." *Billboard* 28 July 1990: 9.

Flohil, Richard. "k.d.: Swingin' into the '90s." *Canadian Composer* Winter 1991: 14.

——. "Voice from the West." *Canadian Composer* Dec. 1985: 4–11, 34–35.

Gillmor, Don. "The Reincarnation of Kathryn Dawn." *Saturday Night* June 1990: 27–35.

Gleason, Holly. Rev. of *Absolute Torch and Twang*, by k.d. lang and the reclines. *Rolling Stone* 13–27 July 1989: 165–66.

"Grammy Win for Singer K.D. Lang." *StarPhoenix* [Saskatoon] 22 Feb. 1990: D4.

Griffin, John. "K.D. Lang Makes Her Big-Screen Debut." *Country* [Ottawa] Dec. 1991–Jan. 1992: 10–11.

Gunnlaugson, Wayne. Telephone interview. 26 Jan. 1992.

Guterman, Jimmy. Rev. of *Angel with a Lariat*, by k.d. lang and the reclines. *Rolling Stone* 16–30 July 1987: 136, 139.

——. Rev. of *Shadowland*, by k.d. lang. *Rolling Stone* June 1988: 121.

Hammond, Marie-Lynn. "Three Sirens of the Absurd: Making Music the Canadian Way." *This Magazine* Aug. 1990: 36–37.

Harrison, Tom. "Country Newcomer." *Province* [Vancouver] 12 Oct. 1984.

Hawthorn, Tom. "Turn Me Round." *This Magazine* Aug.–Sept. 1988: 12–17.

Hayes, David. "A New Prairie Star in Cowboy Boots." *Maclean's* 13 May 1985: 53.

Heatley, Stephen. Telephone interview. 17 Dec. 1991.

Hilburn, Robert. "Did Lang Come to Praise or Parody?" *Los Angeles Times* 1987.

Hodges, Jim. Personal interview. 9 Jan. 1992.

Holden, Stephen. "K.D. Lang's Special Brand of Balladlike Country Rock."

New York Times 14 Aug. 1989: C12.

Hume, Martha. "The Highway of Life: With Loretta Lynn, You're Either on the Bus or on the Bus." *Rolling Stone* 5 May 1977: 56–61.

Ionides, Nicholas. "Lang Cancels: Vegetarian Entertainer Bows to Cow-Country Sentiments." *Globe and Mail* 15 June 1992: C2.

Jennings, Nicholas. "Unchained Melodies." Rev. of *Ingénue* by k.d. lang, and two other albums. *Maclean's* 16 Mar. 1992: S5, S7.

Jennings, Nicholas, and Anne Gregor. "A Bracing Breeze from Western Canada." *Maclean's* 30 May 1988: 58–59.

Jennings, Nicholas, and Celina Bell. "Riding High on a Down-Home Revival." *Maclean's* 3 Aug. 1987: 50–51.

Johnson, Terry. "Alberta Gold." *Alberta Report* 16 Nov. 1987: 58.

Johnson, Terry, and Lori Cohen. "Cowboy Folk and Hootenanny Punk." *Alberta Report* 28 Sept. 1987: 36–37.

Joseph, Frank. "Waylon Jennings: He Shook Country to the Core." *Guitar Player* Jan. 1984: 24–33.

k.d. lang: Ingénue. Narr. Terry David Mulligan. Exec. prod. Moses Znaimer. Prod. Jim Shutsa. Ed. Bill Welychka. MuchMusic Special Presentation. MuchMusic Network. 14 Apr. 1992.

"K.D. Lang Scores Contract Coup, Then Sets Off to Conquer Japan." *Canadian Composer* Oct. 1985: 40.

Kohanov, Linda. "Natural Woman: k.d. lang." *Pulse!* Apr. 1992: 72–77.

Krupp, Charla. "The Amazing k.d. lang: Yahoo!" *Glamour* Feb. 1990: 124.

Lacey, Liam. "Country's Punk Queen." *Globe and Mail* 1 Nov. 1984: E3.

Laderoute, Bette, ed. "People." *Maclean's* 15 Oct. 1984: 42.

"Lang Album Goes Gold as K.D. Makes TV Special with Roy Orbison and Friends." *Canadian Composer* Nov. 1987: 44.

"Lang Happy with Reaction to Recent Admission." *StarPhoenix* [Saskatoon] 11 June 1992: D4.

lang, k.d. *Harvest of Seven Years (Cropped and Chronicled).* Videocassette. Dir. and ed. Jim Gable. Sire Records/Warner Reprise Videos, 1991. 19 songs plus commentary.

——. *Ingénue.* Sire/Warner Brothers, CD 26840, 1992.

——. "The k.d. lang Interview." *Starweek* 11–18 Nov. 1989: 9–12.

——. *k.d. lang's Buffalo Cafe.* Writ. k.d. lang. Exec. prod. Sandra Faire and Larry Wanagas. Prod. Sandra Faire. Prod. of CBC Television, Bumstead Productions, and Sandra Faire Productions, 1989.

——. "Lesley Gore on k.d. lang . . . and Vice Versa." *Ms.* July–Aug. 1990: 30–33.

——— . *Shadowland*. Sire, 92 57241, 1988.

——— . "So in Love." *Red Hot + Blue*. Various artists. Chrysalis, F2 21799, 1990.

lang, k.d., and the reclines. *Absolute Torch and Twang*. Sire, CD 25877, 1989.

——— . *Angel with a Lariat*. Sire, 92 54411, 1987.

——— . *a truly western experience*. Bumstead, BUM 842, 1984.

"Lang's Home Town up in Arms." *StarPhoenix* [Saskatoon] 10 July 1990: C5.

Lemon, Brendan. "Virgin Territory: Music's Purest Vocalist Opens Up." *The Advocate* 16 June 1992: 34–36, 38, 40, 42, 44, 46.

Letters to the editor. *Alberta Report* 13 Aug. 1990: 3–4.

Lomax, John III. *Nashville: Music City USA*. New York: Abrams, 1985.

Lomax, John III, and Robert K. Oermann. "The Heavy 100 of Country Music." *Esquire* Apr. 1982: 65–70.

Magnuson, Ann. "Ann Magnuson Talks while K.D. Croons." *Elle* May 1992: 80, 82, 86.

Mason, Michael, ed. *The Country Music Book*. New York: Scribner's, 1985.

McCall, Michael. "Canadian Singer Shows Hint of Country's Future." *Nashville Banner* 26 Mar. 1987.

McKenna, Kristine. "Midnight Cowgirl: Grammy Award-Winning Country Singer k.d. lang Changes Her Tune on Her New Album, 'Ingénue.'" *Us* May 1992: 46–47, 50–51.

Mitchell, Rick. "Roots and Revival: The Bakersfield Sound." *Musician* July 1989: 58–62, 118.

Muretich, James. "Not Your Average Country Newcomer . . ." *Calgary Herald* 22 Mar. 1984: D1.

Nash, Alanna. *Behind Closed Doors: Talking with the Legends of Country Music*. New York: Knopf, 1988.

——— . "K.D. Lang." Rev. of *Absolute Torch and Twang*, by k.d. lang and the reclines. *Stereo Review* Aug. 1989: 75.

——— . "K.D. Lang's Romantic 'Shadowland.'" *Stereo Review* Sept. 1988: 81.

Naylor, Kathy. Telephone interview. 12 Nov. 1991.

"New Fame for a Soaring Superstar." *Maclean's* 26 Dec. 1988: 14–15.

Oermann, Robert K. "The Nashville Sound." *The Country Music Book*. Ed. Michael Mason. New York: Scribner's, 1985. 84–89.

Pareles, John, and Patricia Romanowski, eds. *The Rolling Stone Encyclo-*

pedia of Rock and Roll. New York: Rolling Stone, 1983.

Philip, Tom, Kenneth Whyte, and Lori Cohen. "The Outrageous K.D. Lang." *Alberta Report* 3 Dec. 1984: 38–45.

Quill, Greg. "Country/Punk Lucy Ricardo Ties One On." *Toronto Star* 1 Nov. 1984: B4.

Remple, Byron. "The New K.D. Lang." *Alberta Report* 23 Oct. 1989: 50–51.

Riese, Randall. *Nashville Babylon: The Uncensored Truth and Private Lives of Country Music's Stars*. New York: Congdon, 1988.

Rogers, Sheila. "k.d. lang: Singing into a Mirror." *Musician* Apr. 1992: 36–43.

Ross, Sean. "No Absolutes for Lyle and Lang: Country PDS Resist Grammy Winners." *Billboard* 10 Mar. 1990: 14, 85.

Scott, Jay. "Yippee-1-0 k.d.! *Chatelaine*'s Woman of the Year." *Chatelaine* Jan. 1988: 54–55, 130–32.

Sievert, Jon. " 'Closer to the Flame'. . . Dave Edmunds' Powerhouse Platter." *Guitar Player* July 1990: 42–52.

Stanley, Shelagh, and Lee Anne Nicholson. "Country Music Sings a New Tune." *Canadian Living* Nov. 1989: 38–39, 41, 43, 45.

Stern, Perry. "k.d. lang Opens Up." *Canadian Musician* Dec. 1988: 48–49.

——. "Sustaining the Edge." *Canadian Musician* Apr. 1987: 28–31.

Stevenson, Jane. "Lang Says Music Her 'Whole Reason for Being.' " *StarPhoenix* [Saskatoon] 27 June 1992: E5.

——. "Lang Says She's Gay, Magazine Reports." *Globe and Mail* 1 June 1992: A12.

Stevenson, Mark. "K.D. the Cow-Hugger." *Alberta Report* 9 July 1990: 19–20.

Straessle, Carla. "Long on Lang." *Flare* May 1986: 62.

Taubin, Amy. "Dial M for Mother." *Village Voice* 16 Oct. 1990: 49.

Taylor, Peter Shawn. "K.D. Lang Sings a Sour Note." *Alberta Report* 23 July 1990: 32–35.

Tosches, Nick. *Country: Living Legends and Dying Metaphors in America's Biggest Music*. Rev. ed. New York: Scribner's, 1985.

Wanagas, Larry. Telephone interview. 10 Feb. 1992.

——. Telephone interview. 13 June 1992.

Weiss, Marc. "Lang Carries a Torch for Country." *Los Angeles Herald Examiner* 4 Apr. 1987: B1, B5.

Wood, Gerry. "Canada's k.d. lang Gains Acceptance." *Billboard* 26 Sept. 1987: 36.

Zimm. Concert rev. of k.d. lang and the reclines. *Variety* 15 Apr. 1987: 210.

Zwarum, Suzanne. "Women to Watch in Alberta." *Chatelaine* Oct. 1986: 85–86, 88.